The Practitioner's Guide

The Practitioner's Guide

Building City
Gospel Movements

By Tom White

Copyright © 2013 by Tom White

PUBLISHING

Published by Good Place Publishing
180 South Avenue
Tallmadge, OH 44278
330-634-2701
www.goodplacepublishing.com

First Printing, September, 2013
Printed in the United States of America

All rights reserved. No part of this publication may be reproduced, stored in a retrieval system, or transmitted in any form or by any means—for example, electronic, photocopy, recording, internet—without the prior written permission of the authors. The only exception is brief quotations in printed reviews.

ISBN: 978-0-939320-25-7

Scripture taken from the HOLY BIBLE, NEW INTERNATIONAL VERSION. Copyright © 1973, 1978, 1984 International Bible Society. Used by permission of Zondervan Bible Publishers.

Table of Contents

Endorsements v

Dedication ix

Forward xi

Prologue 01

  1. Desire and Design to Dwell 11

  2. Laying Out the Blueprints 33

  3. "City Church:" Biblical? Achievable? 53

  4. Leadership Wineskins For City and Regional Movements 75

  5. Putting Citywide Leadership in Place 95

  6. Expanding Collaborative Kingdom Partnerships in Your City 121

  7. Looking Out Ahead: Trends in the City Transformation Paradigm 147

  8. Discerning and Dealing with High Level Spiritual Darkness in your City 173

Epilogue 209

About the Author 223

Appendix 227

Footnotes 279

Endorsements

"*The Practitioner's Guide to Building City Gospel Movements* tackles many of the key issues faced by anyone who believes that Jesus' prayer in John 17 for our unity was meant to be fulfilled by his followers. Tom White's deeply personal journey with city leadership teams reveals accessible principles grounded in experience. The book presents a balanced, viable model for developing a covenant community of leaders who can lift a vision for the whole church taking the whole gospel to the whole city."

    Glenn Barth, Executive Director, Good Cities,
    Author of *The Good City: Transformed Lives Transforming Communities*

I most appreciate books that blend the passion of a theologian with the objective world of practitioners. Being one of the practitioners quoted in Tom White's book, I'm delighted to see a book that deals with the essential foundations of urban "kingdom communities."

The author readily admits that though the strategy for building unity in the Body of Christ takes a variety of approaches, each differing according to the uniqueness of each culture and the work of the Holy Spirit, the increase and urgency of John 17 unity worldwide is undeniable. White offers us plausible and compelling reasons to engage a more holistic approach to collaboration in our cities.
    Rev. Axel Nehlsen, Director, Together for Berlin, Germany

"It has been my privilege to have shared with Tom White for nearly two decades in a variety of ministry settings. I believe that Tom is one of the most gifted prayer and city ministry leaders of our generation. He is uniquely qualified and prepared by the Holy Spirit to share these powerful and practical insights on sharing the Gospel in and through collaborative city movements. I highly recommend Tom and this volume to you."
    Paul Cedar, Chairman, Mission America Coalition

I personally know of no other gospel city movement practitioner who has spent more time on-the-ground serving and investing his life into spiritual leaders across the country and globally over the past 30 years than my friend Tom White. In the Spirit of true humility, Tom brings these decades of experience in tandem with his gifts of leadership and discernment to help birth and sustain leadership teams to impact cities. He has mentored me

Endorsements

personally and helped shape the work of God in Kansas City. If you have a longing to see an increase in kingdom unity, prayer and mission in your city this book will be food for your soul and a practical guide for the journey.

> Pastor Gary Schmitz, Executive Director, Citywide Prayer Movement Kansas City, & Caring for Kids Network

"In this book, Tom White presents not only the biblical foundation for a city reaching movement but gives practical hands on tools and frontline examples that only someone with boots on the ground could do. Tom definitely has the gift of *'unstuck-ness'* that helps give 'traction' to those seeking to advance His Kingdom in their communities. This is a must read for any leader attempting to maneuver through the complexities of a city gospel movement."

> Roger Rutter, Director, Kingston Transformation Network, Ontario, Canada

Tom White shares a wealth of wisdom, experience, and passion for bringing the Body of Christ together for kingdom impact in a city. *The Practitioner's Guide* is a great resource for all city movement leaders and others who want to be part of what God is doing in their cities.

> Chip Sweney, Executive Leadership Team, Next Gen and Community Transformation Division Director, Perimeter Church

Practical, reasonable - I've begged for this book for years. As a "hands on" participant in a decade-long city movement, this *Practitioner's Guide* has given me fresh hope and vision. Why? It's given me a clear framework and calming perspective on what real city movements are and how they work. I also needed and got advice on how to navigate the problems guys like me face as we attempt to build coalitions and movements in our city: like building functional leadership and unity among a diverse body of Christ, the role of prayer and spiritual warfare, how to engage emerging leaders and how to foster humility and sustainability in the movement. Read this for the latest breakthrough reading on city movements.

Andy Rittenhouse, Domestic Missions Pastor,
First Baptist Concord.

I had hardly started reading the Prologue when I knew I was connecting with the Father's heart for His church. This is a practical book with Tom drawing on years of worldwide ministry experience. A must read for those involved in city reaching to grasp a key imperative of God's will for the twenty first century church.

Ian Shelton, Director, One Heart for the Nation,
Toowoomba, Australia

Dedication

In the course of decades of work on the ground in a multiplicity of cities and cultures, an innovator/practitioner such as I have had the privilege of working alongside many of the hidden, unsung heroes and heroines of the city movement world. These are dedicated brothers and sisters who have taken Jesus' Upper Room discourse seriously, and sown their lives into a local community, neighborhood or sphere of cultural influence by living an incarnational witness of John 17 oneness.

To you I dedicate any lasting fruit that comes forth from the message of *The Practitioner's Guide*. I honor you for faithfully stewarding God's astounding grace in the face of all manners of misunderstanding and opposition. Though mostly unheralded, you have the incalculable satisfaction of seeing a healthy Body of Jesus Christ working together to more effectively win and disciple your city. Your true reward will be your "Well done, good and faithful servant," when you reach the city that is yet to come.

As a veteran, boots-on-the-ground practitioner, I thank you for your inspiration and dedication, and honor you for your labors.

Forward

After four decades as a city movement practitioner and coach, Tom White is uniquely qualified to write this book. No one else I know of has traveled to as many global cities and observed the paradigm shattering dynamics of what God is currently doing in cities.

This book is timely - it seems that we have entered a new epoch of missions as God is choreographing nations into urban neighborhoods at an historical pace. With breathtaking speed, the Lord of history is allowing us to see in our own lifetimes a remarkably proximate fulfillment of God's promise to Abraham in Genesis 12 to bless all the nations of the earth.

Tom writes this book from many perspectives - his theological perspective on Jesus' passion for the unity of the church comes to life on every page. His eyewitness accounts and missiological perspectives from five continents adds both substance and credibility to his teaching. From a tactical perspective, Tom knows what it takes to practically build out a sustainable, fruit-bearing city gospel movement.

I have come to know and admire Tom up close in the past few years as we have co-labored on Movement Day in New York City. In the first three years of this gathering we have seen more than 3000 leaders from 360 cites gather from around the world to share and learn best practices. In our 2013 trip to Bangalore for the Lausanne Global Leadership Forum, we met and learned together from city movement practitioners from around the world.

In our very first internet meeting of the Global Urban Leadership Learning Community in September 2013, we co-hosted twenty leaders from thirteen nations. God has given Tom an unusual ability to learn from, lean into, and lead leaders from urban contexts around the world.

Tom articulates with authority the foundational dynamics key to any movement - the need for corporate spiritual disciplines, and the creation of a leadership pipeline. In this book Tom provides building blocks on how to foster a movement - fully recognizing the mystery of God sovereignly working to initiate, sustain, and fulfill such movements.

If the world is going to be 70% urban by 2050 and if the United States will be 87% urban by 2030, the implications of this book are profound. We need to expand the ever increasing "great cloud of witnesses" that will love and serve our cites for the sake of Jesus' gospel.

> Rev. Dr. McKenzie "Mac" Pier, founder, Conference Host of Movement Day and CEO of The New York City Leadership Center.

Prologue

"It's Happening!"

Sometimes the most profound things in our lives are simple, surprising, spontaneous. It happened in a small upper room chapel, east of Haifa, Israel, twenty-seven church leaders from the Galilee region, a mix of Messianic Jews and Arab pastors, seeking the Lord. We had just finished a time of worship, the Messianics, in their Birkenstock sandals and T-shirts, singing in Hebrew and dancing with joy, the Arabs, suits, ties, Bibles tucked under their arms, stiff, with hints of a smile. I looked to my left. The eyes of my colleague and co-facilitator Reuven were tearing up. His observation was sweet and simple, "Abba is happy…his little boys are getting along." Friends, in a church world marked by suspicion and fragmentation, where culture seems so often to trump kingdom, imagine for just a moment the joy that stirs our heavenly Father's heart when his children put aside differences of skin color, language, negative history and culture and celebrate the beauty of the love of his Son dwelling in one another.

Four years earlier, in January 1991, God ignited something new in my spirit as I sat alongside Dr. Joe Aldrich ("Dr. Joe") in a Pastors Prayer Summit in Seattle, Washington. Leaders from a variety of theological backgrounds were getting real, confessing sin, bearing one another's burdens, and getting a vision for walking and working together in their region. Walls came down, and bridges built from heart to heart. It was here that I went deeper trying to grasp the depth of gladness in God's heart when we take seriously Jesus' command for us to love one another.

At the time, a shift in my calling was well underway, transitioning from a ministry of teaching on spiritual warfare and seeking the Lord for new direction. Returning home, I shared an unforgettable de-brief with my wife Terri: "I think we're going to spend the rest of our lives promoting Jesus' John 17 prayer for unity in his Body." A primary focus on spiritual warfare ministry is concerned with getting darkness out of individuals and places. I now found myself working with a fresh and compelling application of this in the context of community. We need to turn on the light. Over time darkness will diminish and disperse. In my understanding, this meant a commitment to bringing kingdom leaders together in John 17 covenantal communities, getting their hearts aligned with one another and God's purposes for their cities. I understood less then, but more today, how labor and love intensive "delivering" a community from darkness really is!

In this book we're going to explore together a distinct work I see God's Spirit doing in communities across the world. We'll look at a variety of models, how saints in any given city organize and apply common principles. But if we rightly understand what Jesus taught his disciples in the Upper Room (John 13-17), we will glean some core essentials that contribute to an authentic kingdom community: loving one another, agreement in prayer on the words and will of Jesus, bearing lasting fruit for the Father's glory. Unity in your city may be sparked by any number of things: a conviction among a core of leaders to change the status quo, a crisis or local calamity that compels the Body to work together, a social need that cries out for solutions. However your movement begins, whatever it looks like, whoever leads it and how, I believe we must regard Jesus' teaching as "home base," the spiritual reference point for who we are, and what we do together.

Fast-forward to 1993, another milestone conversation with Terri. "My deepest prayer and personal longing is to see models of authentic kingdom community up and running in three or four cities." This was still a distant hope, a spiritual dream, and not a current reality anywhere I was aware of. As assignments facilitating Prayer Summits were now accelerating, I was quite often inquiring of the Lord, *"Can functional Ephesians 4 unity of the Body of Christ be a reality not only in a congregation or denomination, but in a diverse expression of Christ's Body across a geographic community?"* As I craft these words in 2013, two decades down line, I'm glad to report, *"It's happening!"*

What we are seeing in our day is an extraordinary worldwide emergence of John 17 covenantal kingdom communities. *"It's happening!"* Concrete answers to Jesus' prayer that his followers would embrace one another with affection, reflect the beauty and glory of the three-in-one Godhead, and be irresistibly attractive to a watching world. So, if the Spirit is stirring in you a vision for the health of the wider Body of Christ in *your* backyard, you're reading the right book. If you are convinced that "we are better together" growing God's kingdom in our communities, this is a timely read. And if you agree that joining hearts and hands with fellow sojourners to partner doing **good deeds** for the needy and broken and bringing the **good news** to the lost, I believe this book will put some time-tested tools in your hands.

If what I'm talking about here "hooks your heart," I invite you to join me engaging these questions: What are the core components of a gospel movement in a city that is led by Jesus? What might the Master Builder's blueprints look like for building his house (Eph. 2:22; 1 Pe. 2:4-10)? How do we engage ourselves building a spiritual dwelling that it is sustained over years, decades, bearing maximum fruit for the Lord's glory? What does "one church, many congregations" really look like on the ground?

In asking these questions, let me clarify something. There are, and always will be, strong congregations and organizations with distinctive strengths and gifts. There are, and always will be, differences we share in doctrine and philosophy of ministry. This is a given, a baseline reality. What I am *not* promoting is a lowest common denominator "ecumenical mush," a mixed porridge of a watered down gospel. I *am* promoting an honoring of one another that Jesus spoke so frequently about and prayed so passionately for. Bottom line, this is about walking and working as brothers and sisters in a local community. *This is about a greater fullness of Jesus' joy being released in and through us, "…so that the world will believe." It's hard to improve on the mission statement crafted by the Lausanne movement: "The whole church taking the whole gospel to the whole city." The Practitioner's Guide* explores how this very compelling statement of mission is finding contextual expression and application worldwide in a variety of cities of differing size and cultural complexity.

How to Read this Book

Here's a heads-up on how best to read this book. Of course readers have their own habits of "digging or diving" into what looks most intriguing. But here's a birds-eye view. While a practitioner, at heart I'm a theologian. That bias will be obvious. I find value and wisdom putting in place a solid biblical foundation. Thus, I'm going to begin *The Practitioner's Guide* getting inside God's heart, wrapping *our* hearts around his "desire and design to dwell" among his people. This is core, baseline revelation, a relational template relevant for any healthy city church expression. Chapter 2 will lay out a biblical blueprint for our call to advancing the kingdom in cities and regions. Chapter 3 anticipates and addresses such questions as, "Is the 'city church' biblical? Why get involved in a citywide movement?" Chapters 4-6 are the "meat and potatoes" of my work, engaging the on-the-ground realities of giving leadership to a local movement, the hard work of forging sustainable, productive partnerships, and the challenge of navigating emerging trends. Some years back, a colleague introduced me to a group of pastors seeking increased unity in their town: "Tom White has the gift of 'unstuck-ness.'" Yes, an odd descriptor. But I would be deeply satisfied if just a few of my inputs serve to help your community get *un-stuck* and growing to a new level.

In Chapter 7, I take my best shot reading trends in the city transformation paradigm, and analyzing the implications of those trends. Chapter 8 brings some distinctive material you'll not find in most books on this topic. One of my areas of expertise is discerning and dealing with spiritual warfare. With city movements in view, here's my premise: if you get increasingly intentional advancing God's kingdom on your knees with your colleagues, you will likely draw negative attention from our common enemy. This content will provide a deeper understanding of this battle, and tools for discerning and pressing through it. Finally, the Epilogue returns full circle to the consideration of God's heart, and highest purpose, re-visiting the inquiry from the Lord himself, *"Where is the house you will build for me? Where will my resting place be?" (Is. 66:1).* At deepest levels, what is our envisioning and energy really about when we casually toss this "transformation" word around? And what might this look like in current reality? Certainly not a pie-in-the-sky utopia. Rather, this is really about a Father looking for a place to settle and dwell among his children.

I'd like to give you a brief exercise.

The following graphic "A Leadership Roundtable Matrix

Prologue

for City or Regional Transformational Movements," has proven helpful for getting many city movements off dead center ("unstuck"), and growing to the next level. This is how I envision a practical, workable releasing of our Lord's "Royal Priesthood" (1 Pe. 2) across a city or regional context. I will give considerable time in Chapter 5 to unpacking and explaining this matrix. King Arthur, whether historical or mythical, had his famous roundtable. But it included only elite, select Knights. King Jesus calls *all* to his table. Pause a moment, peruse this graphic, and envision what a "round table" of kingdom leadership might look like in *your* community.

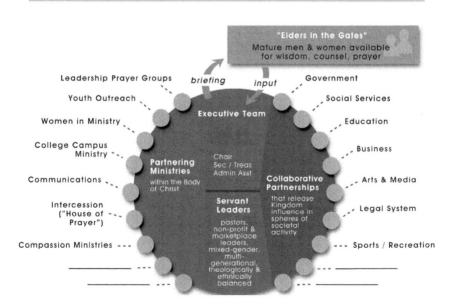

For larger graphic, see the appendix page 279

Does this picture get your attention? Some of you may already be thinking of specific co-laborers in *your* city who should have a seat at this table! As you engage the content of the first four Chapters, I suggest you use this graphic as a template for more intentionally recruiting and releasing the Father's Royal Priesthood in your city! We'll return to this matrix in more detail in Chapter 5 and unpack its contextual implementation.

Here's a closing perspective.

While this Prologue may already be stirring and inspiring you, walking this journey out is a delicate dance. What do I mean by this? If this kind of unity is going to be a movement, it has to be birthed and sustained by the Lord himself. That said, he also calls us, and trusts us, to partner with him. So, we put our hands to the plow, show up for duty, and bring our unique callings and gifts to the mix. But the best of our endeavors must be continually submitted and committed to the sovereign guidance of the Holy Spirit. Solomon, a man who logged as much "on-the-job" training as any man in history, got it right: *"Unless the Lord builds the house, its builders labor in vain. Unless the Lord watches over the city, the watchmen stand guard in vain"* (Ps. 127:1).

Since coming into the kingdom through the "Jesus movement" of the 1960's, I have longed to be a part of an authentic move of God's Spirit. In 1972, in San Diego, I sat at the feet (literally, in an overflow classroom!) of Dr. J. Edwin Orr, the world's leading expert on "revival." This man was a living repository of divine wisdom, sharing a balance of Scriptures and stories when life in a community/region/

nation dramatically changed from ordinary to extraordinary: *the manifest power of God present to transform people and bring human culture back under kingdom reign,* even if for a short span of time. As I sat at this master's feet, listening and soaking, a cry in my spirit began to awaken. A quotation attributed to A. W. Tozer captures this cry. Here's a paraphrase: "Anything God has done any time, he can do *now*. Anything God has done anywhere, he can do *here*. And anything God has done for anyone, he can do with *me (us)*."

I witness readily with the word of the Lord to his people, delivered through Isaiah:

> *"Forget the former things; do not dwell on the past. See, I am doing a new thing! Now it springs up; do you not perceive it?"* Isaiah 43:18, 19

Never in church history have we seen such a longing and stirring for authentic John 17 community in cities and regions worldwide. A fresh favor and grace of God is springing up before our eyes. Do you perceive it? Is this stirring in your spirit? Are you ready to receive it?

This is a book about amazing things that can happen when Jesus' followers, dwelling daily in community, walk and work together, co-laboring to advance the kingdom. This is not about going solo. This is not a mission for mavericks. This is about sons and daughters bringing joy to a father's heart by getting along, following in Jesus' footsteps and being about the Father's business.

Chapter One

Desire and Design to Dwell

In my early years of ministry, I loved to explore and wrestle with theological issues. But as my journey unfolded, I found I was more of a "boots-in-the-mud" practitioner. Before we move too quickly to the nuts and bolts of birthing and building models of John 17 covenantal kingdom communities, I want to offer an over-arching spiritual context that will serve to guide the best efforts of our creative thinking and well intended activity. I want first to zoom out and get a broader "google map" view of our topic. Ponder with me the implications of an amazing inquiry our Lord posed to his people through Isaiah:

> "This is what the Lord says, 'Heaven is my throne, and the earth is my footstool. Where is the house you will build for me? Where will my resting place be? Has not my hand made all these things, and so they came into being?' declares the Lord. 'This is the one I esteem; he who is humble and contrite in spirit, and trembles at my word.'" Is. 66:1, 2b

Seriously, what satisfaction might the God who made heaven and earth derive from a physical place? Having brought all things into being, he could choose any bright, pleasant corner of creation in which to dwell. He chooses instead to reside with humble, self-abasing people. Here's a personal paraphrase: "I prefer to be around a humble heart and contrite spirit more than some magnificent place of splendor!" *God surprises us with an almost inconceivable condescension. He who dwells in lofty places desires to dwell in lowly places.* Here's some further light on this: "I live in a high and holy place, but also with him who is contrite and lowly in spirit, to revive the spirit of the lowly and to revive the heart of the contrite" (Is. 57:15).

Earlier on in the redemptive history of Israel, God made the conditions of his covenantal relationship clear. Obedience brings blessing, rebellion a plethora of painful consequences. But let's notice the central core of his communication to and through Moses:

> "I will look on you with favor and make you fruitful and increase your numbers, and I will keep my covenant with you…I will put my dwelling place among you, and I will not abhor you. I will walk among you and be your God, and you will be my people." Lev. 26:9, 11, 12

I believe a single word captures this message: "nearness." Yahweh gives us a model of relational intimacy. Even with the revelation of the Ten Commandments and other laws, God's intent is not to paint humankind into a corner of legalism, but rather to provide a way for fallen human beings to learn to walk with him. "I will put my dwelling place among you." Pause and think a moment how profound this really is, a perfectly holy and self-sufficient Creator condescending to enjoy fellowship with the imperfect product of his creative handiwork. So, as we begin this book, let's understand that what we are really talking about here is family, a father wanting to be near and do life with his children, wanting to bless and be a regular part of their lives. This is also about a father deeply interested in the perpetuation of spiritual heritage.

So, here's my bias up front: any movement that is truly transformational must be rooted in this revelation and language of "family," healthy relationships among God's people living in the grace of the Holy Spirit, a doing of life saturated in prayer and covenantal love. Increasingly, I'm hearing queries like this: "Haven't we invested enough time praying and relating? When are we going to *do* something?" I get this. I like traction and action as much as anyone. But I'm just plain stuck on pursuing this priority of incarnational models of real people in real places dwelling together as "family." This is horizontal, real people in real places. But this is also vertical, Father God longing for habitation with his chosen children.

Visitation? Why Not Habitation?

One of the privileges of my calling is the grace gift of occasional "visitation," an unexpected, unmerited manifestation of the Lord's presence during a gathering of believers. Perhaps you know what I'm describing. A "holy hush" gently slips over a group, a "blanket" of presence that stills our spirits and zips our lips. As much as it bends my mind to say it, I'm persuaded that Abba Father really *does* enjoy our company! I remember a prayer gathering I facilitated for kingdom leaders in St. Petersburg, Russia, in a World War II intelligence compound near the border with Finland. There were paintings of half-naked women adorning the walls, and gaudy, decadent chandeliers protruding from a low ceiling. I mused to myself, *"Well, Lord, this isn't a terribly edifying atmosphere for a prayer meeting, now is it?"* As we gathered in the evening, quite suddenly the room was flooded with a palpable presence of God. No one spoke. No one moved. Frankly, it felt presumptive just breathing! Participants began to softly utter the names of Jesus, followed by a gentle, unforced flow of love songs to the Savior. What follower of Christ does not long for these grace gifts of "visitation?"

"Visitation" is a wonderful thing, but any visit is momentary, it passes and becomes a memory. But while our triune Lord gives us such occasional satisfying visits, his clearly stated desire is to "dwell" among his people. "Habitation" is an **infusion** of his very presence into the daily tapestry of the lives of his children, and the **inclusion** of his power into the rhythmic lifestyle of a community of believers. On occasion I step into communities where this seems to be very much in play, a palpable presence not just in an event, gathering, prayer meeting or church service, but an overarching reality of love and koinonia that is remarkably cohesive and immediately contagious. So, here's my passion up front. In the midst of the models, blueprints, nuts-and-bolts and best practices now showing up on the city-reaching landscape, I'm most interested in learning how to cultivate a culture that keeps the door wide open to "habitation." I don't see this as mystical, but rather tangible, with features that are observable, and results that are measurable.

Tent, Tabernacle, Temple

During Israel's post-exodus sojourn, Yahweh instructed Moses to provide a place where he and the people could approach him with inquiries, and where he would mediate his presence. Being a people in perpetual motion, Moses first constructed a "Tent of Meeting" outside the camp (Ex. 33:7-11). A manifestation of God's presence, a "pillar of cloud," would descend when Moses entered the tent. At the sight and sign of this, the people worshiped.

Then, careful instructions were given for the construction of a tabernacle, a more elaborate place of meeting, suitable as a dwelling for the ark of the covenant, where he mediated his presence. The instructions for a courtyard, wash basin, lamp-stand, table of showbread, altars of incense and burnt offerings were precise, each purposeful for communing with a holy God. But the heart of the tabernacle was the holy of holies, guarded by a veil, where the ark rested, and where only the High Priest could enter but once every year. Sometimes the Lord's presence would so fill the tabernacle, even Moses could not enter. But in their incessant mobility, changing venues, God's glory in the tabernacle served as a guide, a compass, a cloud by day, a fire by night, "in the sight of all the house of Israel during their travels." Again, the word of the Lord to the people through Moses, "*I will put my dwelling place among you…I will walk among you and be your God, and you will be my people*" (Lev. 26:11, 12). Clearly, this language depicts both the desire and design for habitation, a habitual lifestyle.

Now, one additional piece of Old Testament revelation, Psalm 132, a song descriptive of King David's holy obsession to provide a "dwelling for the Mighty One of Jacob." Once the ark was delivered from captivity among the Philistines, and back in Jerusalem, this incurably passionate lover of Yahweh yearned to provide a more permanent dwelling place for him. The Psalmist speaks of the rumors of the whereabouts of the ark (Ephrathah, or Bethlehem). It was discovered and recovered in the early days of David's reign in Jaar, the "field of woods" (1 Chron. 13:6). So, this Psalm is likely a "popular song" that developed at this time, "Let us go to his dwelling place; let us worship at his footstool" (v. 7). Now, any true worshiper gets this, right? The yearning of the human spirit to commune with its Creator.

But what is most stunning about this song is the next line, "Arise, O Lord, and come to your resting place, you and the ark of your might." Frankly, if we're really honest, this stretches credulity. How can it be that a sovereign, holy God seeks "rest" *anywhere* in the natural realm? And what might attract him to take his own personal Shabbat rest in the midst of his people?

"Favor Factors"

Are there things that God's people, living in any given place, can do to attract a greater measure of his favor, offering him a place to dwell? I believe there are. Let me first dismiss outright a mechanistic understanding of "quid pro quo," we do *this,* and God is obligated to do *that.* Of course there is mystery regarding the interplay between God's sovereign will, and human initiatives, or lack thereof. But it has become clear to me there are things we do that can posture us for increased favor. Here are just a few "favor factors" I have discovered, with reference passages from the Psalms of Ascents and Ephesians. I will describe what I see as attitudes, postures, that are pleasing to the Lord, and serve as holy invitations. While many factors could be touched on here, I want to key in on just four that I see as central.

Submission to the Lord's Sovereignty

Solomon, the man divinely appointed to construct the "resting place" for the Almighty, got it that human effort is futile apart from divine ingenuity and implementation.

> "Unless the Lord builds the house, its builders labor in vain. Unless the Lord watches over the city, the watchmen stand guard in vain." Ps. 127:1, 2

I find it fascinating that Solomon references not only the temple, but also the city of Jerusalem. He goes on to speak of the vanity of toiling--rising early, retiring late. *Here's the point: laboring to accomplish holy endeavors must be empowered by divine inspiration, not human perspiration. The God we seek and serve wants to see not our sweat, but our submission.* I know this will come off to activists as spiritual hype, but what I'm describing does not preclude hands-on servanthood. I'm simply wanting our endeavors anchored in God's grace.

Since the origins of the city-reaching movement, which then morphed into the "city transformation" paradigm around the year 2000, we have seen a wide range of ideas and energy poured into this goal of building citywide movements of unity, prayer and collaboration. As an incurable innovator/practitioner, I have to say, "I love it!" But our highest and most noble intentions can slip into a fleshly zeal that looks great on a glossy whiteboard, but ends up another house of cards. We must keep working Solomon's words through our high energy grids, and regularly submit our labors to the grand Designer of a kingdom that stands the test of time.

The Apostle Paul, given the honor of unveiling God's mystery—the "manifold wisdom" of his plan for the Church—also gets this. He references this plan as being revealed "according to his eternal purpose which he accomplished in Jesus Christ" (Eph. 3:11). Then, in what I consider to be the most inspired and profound prayer offered in the New Testament, Paul begins with this; "For this reason (in view of this amazing plan) I kneel before the Father…" (3:14). Paul models a volitional submission to sovereignty, a recognition of the source of power, through a prayer asking God to make this plan existentially real in the individual hearts and corporate lives of all believers, with an astounding aim: "that you may be filled to the measure of all the fullness of God" (3:19).

Frankly, it exceeds the capacity of the sharpest of human minds to grasp what he is really asking for. This is for us to ponder, pray into, and receive, according to our faith (v. 17). But Paul begins this prayer bowing in awe of the

Almighty, and concludes it by giving all glory to the one "who is able to do immeasurably more than all we ask or imagine, according to his power that is at work within us." So, as we seek to advance God's highest purposes in our cities and nations, let's keep clear that we are simply privileged to be included in on the building of this spiritual house, and check in regularly with the chief Architect!

Intentional Unity

Following in the footsteps of Saul, (a model of fleshly, soulish effort) David faced the Herculean task of re-uniting Israel. And so he addresses citizens of the Northern and Southern kingdoms, who had serious "issues," brothers whose trust had fragmented. Since the inception of the city-reaching movement, Psalm 133 has served as a virtual manifesto of biblical unity.

> "How good and pleasant it is when brothers dwell together in unity!" (Ps. 133:1)

David uses a word in Hebrew that connotes an accentuated strength of emphasis. Literally, it is a good thing when brothers (and, sisters), who have history of conflict, choose to live "together-together!" This is not some superficial, phony accommodation to a King's rule. This is real-deal commitment to put aside differences, and live daily together in authentic kingdom community.

Then David shares two lively similes. This "dwelling" is like precious oil poured out profusely on the head of Aaron the priest, running down his beard, onto his collar and robe. As a sign and symbol of God's blessing through priestly ministry, this is a picture of unmerited favor poured out without measure. But take note. This oil is poured out in response to the commitment of the people of God to dwell "together-together!" This blessing is also likened to the dew, even rain or snow, falling on Hermon, the highest point in Israel, spilling down into the Sea of Galilee, flowing into the headwaters of the Jordan River, and carrying life to the dry places of the land. But here's an interesting observation. David describes this as heavenly dew falling not on Mt. Hermon, but "falling on Mt. Zion," which is the very nexus where earth meets heaven, where God seeks to find rest dwelling with his people!

In 1999, at the close of a Prayer Summit gathering with leaders in Jerusalem, the brothers sat me down, circled around, and began praying for me. As is typical, I expected to see a small vial emerge from a pocket, and a light finger touch my forehead, or the bald spot on the crown of my head (hoping for some supernatural enhancement of my thinning follicles!). Rather, a brother appeared with a large bottle. I first felt the drips descending on my bald spot, then droplets running down my forehead, into my eyes and behind my ears. When I felt it oozing down my neck, I was quite self-conscious, awkward, a bit embarrassed. Then the revelation: when God commands blessing, when he bestows favor, he gives it without measure, without limit, and without regard to human limitations. At this writing, twelve years after this experience, I am more convinced than ever that God is waiting for his people to choose to "dwell together-together," and wanting to pour out an impartation of his blessing that is both unmerited and immeasurable.

"For there," says David, "the Lord bestows his blessing, even life forevermore." An apt synonym for "bestow" is the word command. So, where, and why, does the Lord command such favor? Where his people, who have "stuff," who carry seeds of mistrust in their hearts towards one another, choose to obey the Father's call to live together in harmony. Paul issues a similar call to members of the Church: "be patient, bearing with one another in love. Make every effort to keep (not create!) the unity of the Spirit through the bond of peace" (Eph. 4:2b).

Humility

Imagine David for a moment, the highest ruler of a nation inhabited by people chosen by the Almighty to demonstrate the glory of his plan. This could go to a man's head (as it did with most of the kings who followed David). Imagine the problems and pressures he had to navigate, building a capital city, fending off enemies, developing commerce for his people and daily discerning an endless mix of problems and conflicts. And yet here is the true mark of this man, humility:

> *"My heart is not proud, O Lord, my eyes are not haughty; I do not concern myself with great matters or things too wonderful for me. But I have stilled and quieted my soul; like a weaned child with its mother"* Ps. 131:1, 2

Honestly, it challenges me to imagine David having this mind-set. It is one thing to acknowledge one's dependence on divine wisdom, to embrace humility. But it seems to me quite another to liken oneself to "a weaned child with its mother!" This is a King speaking? David is describing here a volitional restraint from soulish striving: rest, settledness, rooted in humility.

So how does Paul capture this in a New Testament context? "Be completely humble and gentle" (Eph. 4:2), in pursuing relationship with fellow believers. And the parallel word, which we have already looked at, is the "kenosis" passage ("emptying") of Philippians 2:1-11, a call to pattern our lives after Jesus, who "humbled himself, and became obedient to death" for our sakes. And so, in any city movement, if saints get serious putting this spirit into practice, I believe God will manifest his favor in greater measure: "Do nothing out of selfish ambition or vain conceit, but in humility consider others better than yourselves" (2:3). When we choose to prefer the interests of others above our own, this is self-sacrificing love.

This attitude, which dwelt in full measure in Jesus, attracts the Father's pleasure. For you and me, in our mortality, such grace is humanly impossible, unachievable apart from the grace of Jesus Christ filling the heart. And he does, and is doing just that, in city after city, where leaders are willing to embrace the grace of humility. What does this look like? It looks like the pastor of a small, struggling church rejoicing over the growth of another local church or ministry. It looks like a congregation sharing a sacrificial gift to another congregation launching a building expansion. It looks like a gifted leader on a city team stepping aside for a season to make room for another leader to step up and serve. It looks and feels like "family."

Serving the Poor and Marginalized.

This could be the most explicit "favor factor" we find in the Scriptures. In the early 1990's, soaking in Isaiah 58, I became convinced that the revelation of God's compassion for the poor had to be at the heart of authentic kingdom movements in our cities. Yahweh is a God of justice.

> *"Is not this the kind of fasting I have chosen: to loose the chains of injustice and untie the cords of the yoke, to set the oppressed free and break every yoke? Is it not to share your food with the hungry and to provide the poor wanderer with shelter—when you see the naked, to clothe him, and not to turn away from your own flesh and blood?" (Is. 58:6, 7)*

If we take this revelation seriously, and engage ourselves caring for the poor and downtrodden, God blesses us with supernatural favor: "*Then* your light will…dawn. Your healing will quickly appear; *then* your righteousness will go before you, and the glory of the Lord will be your rear guard." The "if-then" parallel is clear. There is just no way the most gifted practitioners of movements of prayer and unity can produce results this tangible! The Lord says he will also more quickly answer our prayers, and make us shine like blazing lights in the surrounding darkness. His blessings herein described are profuse and profound. I will not offer a full exposition, only to capture one line: "You will be like a well-watered garden, like a spring whose waters never fail" (58:11b). The language here, in ancient near-Eastern thinking, depicts a bubbling up of happiness. This is tangible prosperity, fruitfulness.

And then the language remarkably shifts to the imagery of re-building a broken-down city: "Your people will re-build the ancient ruins and will raise up the age-old foundations; you will be called Repairer of Broken Walls, Restorer of Streets and Dwellings" (58:12). This is an invitation to return to our Lord's original kingdom reign, to be re-established on the foundation of God's covenantal promises. "You will ride upon the high places." The language depicts a conqueror riding in a chariot following success in battle. The Lord is saying, "I will give back to you your land, the heritage of Jacob, and you shall occupy and prosper." And, consistent with his original call to Abraham, the restoration of Israel would also serve as a light to the Gentile nations.

It seems clear to me that when God's people are willing to be conduits of good deeds, they become the incarnation of good news. Again, let's steer clear of the "quid, pro, quo" mentality, "we do this, he will do that." But I believe we can build a culture where we understand favor factors, build in spiritual rhythms that draw the Father's pleasure, and live in expectancy.

Building Covenantal Kingdom Community

Over the years I have had the joy of facilitating well over seven hundred Leaders Prayer Summits worldwide among a variety of cultures and language groups. Whatever the length of time, and whatever it is called, drawing apart with God is a vital component to building community. This is a corporate Shabbat, an intentional break in our frenetic pace of life, a simple format of leaders taking time to seek the Lord. While this is only one approach, it has proven to be effective in numerous city movements worldwide. It really doesn't matter what you call it, or how long it is. What does matter is that busy leaders take time to "get out of Dodge City" and be kingdom family. This, I believe, opens a door for the grace of sustained "habitation."

In many Summits and retreat settings I have brought a visual demonstration to answer an oft-asked question, "Why are we doing this?" I line up five chairs, and ask for five volunteers. Dr. Joe Aldrich, founder of the Pastors Prayer Summit movement in 1989, is the originator of this core progression. So, picture five leaders, sitting in chairs at the front of a room.

CHAIR #1	CHAIR #2	CHAIR #3	CHAIR #4	CHAIR #5
Extended Time In God's presence	Humility	Unity	Healthy Kingdom Community	Revival, Awakening, Transformation
(Ps. 27:4)	(Eph. 4:2)	(Eph. 4:3)	(Eph. 4:15, 16)	(Ps. 85:4-7)

I begin standing behind Chair # 5, tracing back from our highest desired outcome, to core initiatives required to get there. Whatever language one may use, Chair #5 is a longing to see God lift us out of our ordinary, best-effort endeavors, and display his extraordinary grace. I like describing this as an "open heaven." Traditionally, most of us are familiar with the terms "revival," or "awakening." And we know, in response often to desperate prayer, the Lord *does* manifest his presence in particular places, for seasons of time. For example, the powerful preaching and conversions under John Wesley and George Whitfield in England in the 1840's, the unusual anointing on Charles Finney in the Eastern United States, the revival in Wales in the early 1900's. As a student trained at Asbury Seminary I arrived in Wilmore, KY in 1973, two years following a sovereign move of the Spirit that began at the close of a chapel service at Asbury College, and spread quickly around the Southeast US.

Here's the question. Can saints living in any community or region do anything to qualify for God's supernatural work of transformation? Can we posture ourselves for outpouring? Having shared earlier four "favor factors" that help to open a door to divine grace, I believe yes. And in view of my own personal journey, I want to return to Chair # 1, a context in which we spend extended and undistracted time in God's presence. Will we take time to offer God a "resting place?" Having a resolve to gear down from distractions and ministry duties, and sit at the Lord's feet, and allow him to speak and set our agenda, is the place to begin. Frankly, we all get caught so easily in the gears of cultural busyness. I believe we must regularly submit our type A personalities, shake off our common cultural compulsions, embrace Shabbat, welcome God's rest and take time to wait. Time and time again, over thirty years on this journey, I have watched the Holy Spirit gain fresh access to distracted hearts.

When the Spirit brings genuine conviction, exposing misplaced priorities, sins of presumption, sin in our relationships or behavior, he begins to purge pride and self-sufficiency. There is a breaking that comes in the Lord's presence, the grace of humility, a spirit of contrition. To the extent that I remain obsessed with the demands of ministry, and my attempt to meet them, I remain caught up in the endless machinations of performance. But when I allow my heart to listen to the Word of God, I give the Spirit access, exposing my presumption and self-effort. This is Chair # 2, a place of extraordinary grace.

In 2005, huddled in a hot upper room in Calcutta with around sixty kingdom leaders, Terri and I were co-facilitating a Prayer Summit. Gently led by the Spirit, we were in worship, singing with just our voices, and watching for where the Lord was guiding. Abruptly, a troubled voice broke in: "Brother White, I don't want to break the flow here, but I just cannot go on. Would you allow me to unburden my heart?" This elder Indian pastor looked straight across the circle at an American church planter: "Brother, I've carried bitterness in my heart towards you for years, for taking some of my best sheep." In ministry, this is as real as it gets. This broke things open. Another brother confessed a spirit of competition with a fellow pastor. Suddenly, in God's mercy, this sweaty sanctuary turned into a place of extraordinary grace. As we moved back into a closing season of worship, Noel, my Indian co-facilitator, leaned over to me: "Brother, this is a breakthrough! This is a highly esteemed leader in Calcutta, and a close personal friend of Mother Teresa."

Here's the point. It is impossible to move towards Chair # 3, authentic unity, without first embracing the grace gift of humility. To the extent that God "pulls my plug" of pride, presumption and ambition, and empties me of self-interest, to that extent will I be able to honor and prefer other brothers and sisters as more important than myself, even desiring their success and fruit in ministry above my own. When Paul exhorts you and me to "be completely humble," this assumes we possess the capacity to yield to the work of the Spirit to do an "extreme makeover" in our interior lives. And it is this kind of "interior remodeling" that I see God do in the hearts of men and women around the world, gracing them to "make every effort to keep the unity of the Spirit through the bond of peace" (Eph. 4:3).

We don't create unity. It is a spiritual grace that we receive, and maintain. But we can only receive when we renounce our pride, prejudice and criticism of others. And *when we give ourselves to extended times with God and one another, he humbles us. When this happens in repetitive gatherings, and is reinforced by leaders in a city engaging in regular times of prayer, authentic kingdom culture is developed.* Over time, we steward and strengthen this culture. This is true koinonia, a gift of life that we perpetuate through obedience. In Corvallis, we've been praying every Thursday since April, 1999. If you were to drop into "CitiPrayer," I believe you would experience spontaneous, unforced koinonia--pastors, leaders of ministries, men, women, intercessors, marketplace leaders-- "making every effort" to steward the grace gift of oneness in Jesus' love. This should not just be a remote possibility, but a reality, a "new normal" of vibrant kingdom life.

To conclude, Chair # 4, healthy kingdom community, becomes a goal in any city or region that is both attainable and sustainable. Simply stated, God finds a "resting place" among his people who take seriously this matter of regularly offering him a place! *He is interested, and so should we be, not merely in occasional "visitation," but in sustained "habitation" in the hearts of real people in real places.* Biblically, we see this described in Acts 2:42-47, and in the description of the Church in Thessalonica, which Paul commended as a model of authentic kingdom community. He encourages their example: "You became a model to all the believers in Macedonia and Achaia. The Lord's message rang out from you…" (I Thess, 1:7, 8b). We also see a description of the regional Body of Christ "throughout Judea, Galilee and Samaria…strengthened and encouraged by the Holy Spirit" (Acts 9:31). *The Church grew numerically, spontaneously, and lived in the fear of the Lord. This, as I read this verse, is a perfect, simple description of what we're after, God among us, dazzling us daily with the wonder and awe of what he is up to…habitation!*

And when the "one church, many congregations" in a city stewards this over time, they must guard against the complacency of "arriving." We keep praying, believing, and pressing into God's full redemptive destiny for our city or region. And, like the watchmen and watchwomen on Jerusalem's walls (Isaiah 62), we give God no rest, and take no rest, until he accomplishes his highest purposes in our city. This is indeed an unending, multi-generational intercession, a pouring forth of incense that ascends to God's throne until Jesus returns. We keep pressing into the possibility of a wider spiritual awakening that brings the lost into the fold, raises higher the standard of righteousness and increases biblical justice. In "chair #5," we don't sit, but stand in awe of the hand of the Lord bringing true transformation. And we grow in faith that sin strongholds can be broken, prodigals returned to the fold, marriages healed, and the hearts of fathers turned to their children, and children to their fathers. More simply stated, a return to kingdom reign.

"City Transformation:" A Working Definition

Let's unpack what we might really mean by "favor." The term "transformation" has been a major "buzz word" in recent years. With the innovation of "Movement Day" in 2010, we're now talking about "city gospel movements." Language will always adapt to fit culture, but we can be sure that core components of the kingdom remain the same. I have labored in this opening chapter to describe this not as utopia, but rather co-laboring with God to build sustainable expressions of kingdom life in the here-and-now. What we're after is a measurable increase of kingdom influence that is released into all spheres of social activity, what others refer to as the "seven mountains," or "domains" of human society. Again, a variety of language is being employed to describe this. Here's the object of our praying: that God's shalom, the fullness of all he is and all he does as life-giver, would permeate the whole of life in a community.

In closing, I want to offer an operative definition of what I believe we are praying and working towards, my best take on the Lord's desire and design. While the Bible does not explicitly portray the spiritual transformation of a city as a kingdom goal, we can surely labor to invest in places where the influence of kingdom righteousness increases, and the activity of darkness decreases (see Isaiah 65 for our best biblical model for this. Eric Swanson and Sam Williams exposit and expound on this in their seminal work, *To Transform a City*). Thus, "city transformation" can be described as the measurable, sustained impact of the power of God through his people in a particular place that restores both individuals and societal structures towards a kingdom reign. *In the Body of Christ, this is typically characterized by an increase in:*

- -- a lifestyle of humility and holiness
- -- organic oneness and health of relationships
- -- fervent prayer that is regular, united and fruitful
- -- sacrificial, collaborative serving of the lost & the least
- -- generosity resourcing local and global ministries

In the spheres of societal activity, this is characterized by—

- -- increased, pervasive awareness of the presence of God
- -- increase of the percentage of Christians to the general population
- -- measurable correction of social ills, e.g., decrease of crime
- -- reduction of the destructive power of demonic and institutional evil
- -- increased productivity of local commerce and well-being of employees

"Your people will re-build the ancient ruins and will raise up the age-old foundations; you will be called Repairer of Broken Walls,

Restorer of Streets with Dwellings" (Is. 58:12). Outcomes like this cannot be achieved through government programs, more money and our best manpower. Could anyone aspire to any job description more noble or fulfilling? Friends, this paradigm of God at work in cities and regions is alive and growing. *"It's happening!"* Let's head to the construction site, roll up our sleeves and lay out the blueprints.

Chapter Two

Laying Out the Blueprints

In the late 1970's, I had a dramatic vocational shift. I went into a partnership with a Christian brother building residential houses in Corvallis, Oregon, "Pilgrim Homes." Those were the "boom days," with Hewlett Packard moving a large plant and lots of jobs into town. I played around designing a few homes, and learned the value of a good design and detailed blueprints. But constructing earthly homes was temporary. Joining the ranks of everyday hard workers resulted in God building more character into my life than me building homes (that's the "pilgrim" piece).

You already know I'm enamored not with temporal houses, but with building the house of the Lord, the here-and-now presence of his kingdom in people's hearts. In Chapters 3-6, I'll get down to the nuts and bolts of what it takes to build a life changing, fruit-bearing city gospel movement. But first, a few words about the importance of a spiritual foundation. Dr. Tim Keller, in *Center Church*, describes doctrinal foundations as the "hardware" we need to work with, and ministry programs being the "software." But I like how he depicts "theological vision" as the "middleware" that brings it all together:

> "Between one's doctrinal beliefs and ministry practices should be a well-conceived vision for how to bring the gospel message to bear on the particular culture setting and historical moment.".[1]

So, in this chapter, I'm working on the "middleware." We'll need to glean a few things from Nehemiah, perhaps the wisest and most successful project manager we meet in the Scriptures. While this might seem like an old, familiar Bible story, this portion of Old Testament history gives us an enduring model, with valuable lessons for us today. We need to get what this man was really up to repairing broken walls and burned gates, and how he went about it. As you read, ask the Lord, the Master Builder, for some takeaways for your call to participate in building a city movement in the twenty-first century.

Restoring the Ruins

Continuing on from the theme of Chapter 1, I want to talk a bit about the significance of the original temple, the city where it was placed, and share some implications for New Testament believers. Israel had endured an agonizing exile in Babylon, under the Lord's corrective discipline. In 538, God intervened dramatically. He sovereignly stirred Cyrus, king of Babylon to act on behalf of his people. Further, he placed a mantle of leadership on some men to restore the ruins of Solomon's temple. Ezra, Nehemiah, Haggai, and Zechariah provide us with the account of God's personal project to restore the temple. Over two generations these and others carefully followed his ways, first in restoring the place of his dwelling, and second, the protective wall around it. The Lord raised up Haggai and Zechariah (prophets), Zerubbabel (governor of Judah), Joshua (son of the High Priest) and "the whole remnant of the people (Hag. 1:14) to engage in "Phase I:" restoring the temple, the place of meeting. Some seventy years later, he stirred up Ezra (priest), and Nehemiah (practitioner) to complete "Phase II:" the repair of the broken walls and burned gates. These leaders, over three generations, are prototypical models of spiritual reform—getting God's desire right—and implementing his design.

Haggai and Ezra represent what I would describe as the **"internal component,"** re-kindling the priorities of worship and the Word of God: let's use a familiar term here, "revival." Nehemiah incarnates and models the **"external component,"** the resulting repair of the social and economic conditions of the city: "restoration." In both spheres, it is imperative to grasp that God works through human, flawed agents in the context of space/time reality. In short, holy endeavors are long, sloppy and subject to the sabotage of negative spiritual forces. So, when we look at contemporary experiments, let's understand it may take decades to see the evidence of sustainable impact of sovereign God changing life in a city from brokenness to kingdom reign. In reality, in the United States, some of our more productive models are now reaching thirty years of age.

The Time Line: Rubble to Restoration

For readers with linear minds here's what happened, and when:

> 538   *Stirred by the Spirit, Cyrus decrees the return of the exiles to Jerusalem to rebuild the temple. Zerubbabel and some fifty thousand exiles begin the journey home.*
>
> 536   *The foundation of the temple is completed, and opposition to the project begins to impede progress.*
>
> 522   *Under inspiration of the Spirit, Darius, King of Babylon, issues a decree to continue the temple project, and offers assistance with materials and labor.*
>
> 520   *The prophetic voices of Haggai and Zechariah stir the hearts of the leaders and the people to rise, build, and return to the Lord.*
>
> 516   *The work on the temple is completed.*
>
> 460   *Ezra and Nehemiah return to Jerusalem to oversee the restoration of the walls and the gates, and to call the people back to their spiritual priorities.*

Over roughly eighty years we see the acceleration of God's purpose to restore the broken relationship with his people. This deep, spiritual task is both time and labor intensive. *Let's explore briefly the biblical blueprints from both Old and New Testaments, and the implications this might have for your context.*

Listening to Haggai

Here is the gist of Haggai's message: wake up and get your priorities straight! "This is what the Lord Almighty says: These people say, 'The time has not yet come for the Lord's house to be built'" (Hg. 1:2). Remember, this re-settling comes after a season of incalculable loss and pain, exile under a foreign oppressor, and the absence of familiar geography and culture. So, the Jews were literally re-settling their old homes and neighborhoods, focused on some measure of a return to normalcy. Let's be honest, you and I would have been caught in the same mind-set: "finally, home again!" But the Lord's corrective is clear, concrete: This *is* the time to give attention to your highest spiritual priority.

Then a second warning: "Give careful thought to your ways" (Hg 1:5). He chides them for their preoccupation with their own lives: "Is it a time for you ... to be living in your paneled houses, while this house remains a ruin?" (1:3). Yahweh puts his finger on the pain and non-productivity of independent self-effort, his people doing their own thing, their own way, in their own time. So, you sow, you plant, and the harvest is meager. You eat but are not full, drink but not satisfied, earn wages, only to find holes in your pockets and purses! (1:5-9).

The people hear and receive the rebuke. They "get it," and say "yes" to God's highest desire and design. Amazingly, "the whole remnant of the people obeyed the voice of the Lord ... and the message of the prophet Haggai, because the Lord their God had sent him. And the people feared the Lord"

(1:12). This might seem like an amazing and uncharacteristic response. But remember, these folks have just emerged from two generations of pain, judgment and exile under a foreign oppressor. Thus, they heard, not the voice of a man, but the voice of the Lord. They followed their leaders and put their hands to the task. The Master Builder honors their obedience: "Be strong, all you people of the land, for *I am with you!*" (2:4). When God's people come into alignment, he provides the appointing of skilled leaders and the anointing of grace to accomplish the task. In four years, the temple was restored.

Learning from Ezra

Let's jump ahead about fifty-five years, to Ezra's call to return to Jerusalem. The first six chapters describe the joyous completion of the work of rebuilding the temple. *I find it significant that after the foundation was complete, the altar was given first attention.* Ezra models a quick and unquestioning response to divine initiative: "the good hand of his God was on him" (7:9). This man has authentic humility. He was patient to "wait his turn" before returning to the city and people he loved. He watched for the Lord's purposes to unfold, then followed. Starting the journey with an assortment of adults, children, and probably donkeys and camels laden with earthly "stuff," he refused offers from the king for protection. Instead, the Lord honored his faith and protected his endeavors.

There is something instructive here for us today. It is tempting for a reform-minded person to get impatient, impulsive. Ezra trusted God's timing. He knew that he alone had the blueprint and the schedule for construction. *True spiritual reform requires men and women discerning enough to see the need for change, but dependent enough on God to wait and watch for him to execute it. In our kingdom-building endeavors, may our fingerprints not be found on the living stones of the house of the Lord!*

Here's another encouraging part of the blueprint. Artaxerxes appointed Ezra to oversee the gathering of further provisions for the temple. Before departing Babylon, the exiles celebrated the Passover a full seven days "because the Lord had filled them with joy by changing the attitude of the king of Assyria, so that he assisted them in the work on the house of God" (6:22). *Think about this. When God is at work, we see a remarkable synergy of heaven and earth. A God-ordained favor may open doors to the hearts of secular authorities, who come alongside with political influence and resources.* Currently, worldwide, in numerous cities, secular government officials are recognizing and supporting the value of God's people serving as "salt, light and leaven," a positive and constructive influence. A current "buzz" in city movement circles is "cross-sector collaboration," believers and unbelievers from the private, public and social sectors tackling civic challenges of all sorts. Increasingly, this is even happening in China. A high Confucian value is promoting harmony in one's society. Following the massive 2005 earthquake in Sichuan Province, Christians in Chengdu were first responders, mobilizing and sustaining relief efforts. This quickly got the attention of the Premier of the Communist

Party, and significantly improved the public profile of the Church. Closer to home, in the aftermath of Hurricane Katrina, believers were some of the first to show up, and the last to leave.

Buoyed by the extra support, it was nevertheless Ezra's job to call the people to brokenness before the Lord. As a priest-intercessor, he was willing to stand in the gap between God's holiness and the repetitive sins and stumblings of his people. You may be a pastor, church leader, or an intercessor. As you're watching the Lord's house being raised in your community, be open to opportunities to call people to repentance. Pray for the gift that Ezra was given, the discernment to put a finger on the problem, and the conviction to call people to honestly deal with attitudes or actions that grieve the Lord and stifle his favor. Both Haggai and Ezra, in successive generations, called the people to re-kindle their priority to give attention to the "resting place," the Tent of Meeting, the Tabernacle, the Temple, the place where God could fulfill his covenantal desire: "I will walk among you and be your God, and you will be my people" (Lev. 26:12). This, then, is top priority, giving attention to the "internal component." *For you and me today, this might sound like Jesus' word to backslidden believers in Ephesus: "I hold this against you, you have forsaken your first love…Repent and do the things you did at first" (Rev. 2:4, 5).*

Building with Nehemiah

A contemporary of Ezra, Nehemiah had a high-level position as cupbearer to Artaxerxes, King of Persia. But he got word that the walls of Jerusalem were still broken, and the gates in disrepair after being burned during Nebachudnezzar's invasion. Nehemiah picked up this burden, weeping over the condition of his home city. He brought his burden to the King: "Because the gracious hand of my God was upon me, the king granted my requests" (Neh. 2:8). And so, with the assistance of the King, he traveled to Jerusalem for an on-site inspection. So, what is the spiritual significance of the walls and the gates? Clearly, they served functionally as a perimeter of protection, keeping enemies out, and allowing friends, allies and commerce to come in. This repair was imperative, and timely. It is important to note that in every phase of this assignment, Nehemiah saturated his endeavors with prayer. In crisis after crisis, he regularly "goes vertical" and finds wisdom for every hassle faced in the horizontal.

Approaching the project, Nehemiah inherited a pile of rubble and a host of rabble-rousers. The local ruffians Sanballat and Tobiah ridiculed and scorned the laborers. As work got underway, the people began to lose heart, "there is so much rubble that we cannot rebuild the wall" (4:10). Sometimes, we look at our circumstances, perhaps in a church situation or in assessing the condition of the Body of Christ in our city. Our self-talk may sound something like this: "Lord, what am I to do with all this rubble? This is overwhelming!" It can feel like standing at the site of the World Trade Center 9/11 catastrophe with a shovel and a wheelbarrow. All too often we pick up mutterings and murmurings within the camp, "there is so much rubble ... we cannot rebuild the wall." Voices, words, innuendo, negativism, attitudes that denigrate and de-motivate. "What are these feeble pastors doing? Are all these prayer meetings and forums and service days really worth the time and effort?"

On top of weakness within the faith camp, attacks also arose from outside the camp (Neh. 4:11), enemies taking their shots. What can we learn here? First, the role of the leader is to quiet anxieties and bolster confidence: "Don't be afraid of them. Remember the Lord, who is great and awesome, and fight" (Neh. 4:14). Confident of his calling and assignment, Nehemiah wisely placed the workers on the wall according to their strengths. He picked out those skilled in hand-to-hand combat, men with physical prowess, and made them soldiers. As leaders, we must put men and women on the perimeter endowed with discernment, courage, and authority to "stand watch." There are implications in the text that people labored in areas literally adjacent to their own, original neighborhoods. No doubt this stirred increased local ownership and responsibility.

And second, he employed a strategy: "Whenever you hear the sound of the trumpet, join us there. Our God will fight for us!" (4:20). *Sometimes in the day-to-day battles, it is comforting to know that friends of like heart and call are posted on the wall, "watching your back."* The shofar serves as both a call to war, and to prayer. This sound was a call to rally at a particular place on the wall. When we gather in a city for prayer and worship, we may stand in the gap for specific areas of vulnerability. Sometimes we need to lift up a church in trouble, or give cover to an embattled colleague. We may need to pray over divisive issues and disputes in our local government, or intercede in the aftermath of a local crime, such as a school shooting, or mobilize in response to a natural calamity. As the moral fabric of our culture may be unraveling, it is the role of God's people to be about repairing and restoring.

A Call to the Wall

Today our cities have no physical walls or identifiable gates. But as the New Covenant Royal Priesthood, I suggest we carry a responsibility to maintain a spiritual wall around the places we call home. In the New Covenant, the collective Body of Christ is the temple, the locus of God's presence (Eph. 2:22). Thus, the component most vital to a city's well-being is a healthy, praying, serving church. We are a living society, corporate and organic, through which our Lord's favor and shalom are mediated to all peoples dwelling in that place. So, if we, living stones, are the temple, then what is the wall? Where are the gates? *Here's what I have come to believe: our obedience to worship together, our commitment to walk in righteousness, our zeal to love one another, our intercessory prayers for the people and places where we dwell, all of these release God's shalom into the city:* peace (harmony, well-being), protection (reduction of crime, drug and sex trafficking, injustice) and prosperity (growth of commerce, provision of jobs). This is why God gives the following instruction to Israel, in exile in a foreign land:

> *"Seek the peace and prosperity of the city to which I have carried you in exile. Pray to the Lord for it, because if it prospers, you too will prosper" (Jer. 29:7).*

Yes, the Body of Christ in a city serving as walls and gates is a metaphor. But I do believe the Church of the city carries a responsibility to provide spiritual protection where she dwells, worships and works. As citizens of heaven, pilgrims "just passing through," we are *all* exiles in the cities where we dwell! If we falter or fail in our responsibility to walk in righteousness and to pray God's shalom into our cities, the walls and gates are vulnerable. The sin and spiritual sloth of the saints may give our enemies legal right to bring such pollutants as injustice, greed, violence, and sensuality through cracks in our walls and holes in our gates.

For you and me, facing today's current realities, repairing the wall involves dealing honestly with issues of strife and disunity in our congregations, roots of unforgiveness and bitterness in relationships, rampant adultery and divorce in our own ranks, sexual promiscuity among our people, and compromise with cultural idolatries. It is about admitting that in reality we are not seeking first God's face, but rather getting caught up in cultural snares of all sorts. *How can we presume on God to shield us and give favor to our endeavors when our spiritual house is in disarray? I believe the Body of Christ carries a corporate responsibility for the wellbeing of our cities.*

Honest Assessment

Neither naysayers nor idealists are well suited to serve as reformers. We need leaders like Nehemiah, who can remove the rose-colored glasses, assess reality for what it is, then approach the problem with concerted prayer and hope in our Redeemer. I've been in cities where the rubble of apathy, disunity, and unbelief is overwhelming. Often there is a long-standing root of bitterness in a church of influence tracing back to the painful departure of a pastor, or a church split. A spirit of strife and division is often exported to other churches in the community. Someone needs to rightly discern ill-health in the local Body of Christ, and the vulnerability it brings to a city. Before any medical doctor can offer an effective remedy, he must have an accurate diagnosis. We need those who can see the cracks in our city walls, and holes in the gates.

Prayer Itself Is the Strategy

As I'm writing this book, we're entering a strong cycle of activism. Prayer? Building relationships? Repentance? Been there, done that. Here's my take. If we're really about the Father's business, whatever phase we find ourselves in, prayer will always be a priority, even concurrent with events and service projects. *Desperate prayer that keeps us dependent is the single most enduring component of God's blueprint for rebuilding abandoned altars and broken walls.* Nehemiah cultivated a life of prayer. He was postured to hear and receive the Lord's burden, read his timing and discern his wisdom for a challenging, complicated project.

Actually, we can say that prayer itself seems to have been Nehemiah's chief strategy. When frustrated, fearful, or facing opposition, he prayed. When the "gruesome twosome" Sanballat and Tobiah scorned the project and spit in Nehemiah's face, he prayed (4:4). He didn't get caught in the snares of back-and-forth insults. He didn't spit back at the mockers. He asked the Lord to turn the scorns back on themselves. Recognizing the opposition is not really directed at *him,* he turned the tormentors over to divine judgment. As a result of his leadership, the people re-engaged the work in earnest. The gruesome twosome come back at them, this time with the "Triple A" mob, "the Arabs, the Ammonites and the men of Ashdod" (4:7), angry and plotting a riot to shut it all down. Nehemiah "goes vertical" (not ballistic!): "we prayed to our God and posted a guard day and night to meet this threat" (4:9). *Opposition was turned into an opportunity for Yahweh Jireh to demonstrate his sovereign power.*

Understanding Spiritual Components of "The Wall"

So, what can Ezra, Nehemiah and Old Testament prophets offer today's innovators seeking to incarnate the kingdom of God in a post-Christian culture? I see two clear takeaways from Nehemiah, a restoration of righteous living, and an active renunciation of injustice.

Returning to Righteousness.

In his closing plenary at Movement Day in September, 2012, Dr. Tim Keller quoted theologian Leslie Newbigen, sharing that the Church must serve as both a "contrast community, and a prophetic community." In brief, we need to stand up and stand out more as we accelerate into a post-Christian milieu. In this light, we need a better grasp of the significance of this spiritual wall around the cities we find ourselves living and working in today. In the midst of repairing the walls and gates, Nehemiah exposed a local sin stronghold, and railed at the Jewish hierarchy for it (see Neh. 5). Finding themselves in famine, people had been forced to mortgage their land to secure food, to borrow funds to pay the king's tax, even to sell their children into slavery. Nehemiah confronted the sins of usury and slavery, demanding they stop. People emptied their own pockets to relieve the burden of the underprivileged. To free up additional resources for the people, Nehemiah refused to receive the allotment of food and provisions normally provided a governor. Here is the implication and application for some of the societal crises we face today: the Body of Christ is responsible to confront and help correct social injustice. As Americans, we've got plenty of it: the repetitive greed of Wall Street, the sexualization of our culture, human trafficking, tampering with God's definition of marriage, to name a few.

Returning to one of the "favor factors" we looked at in Chapter 1, the Lord wants to empower his people to be the "Repairer of Broken Walls, Restorer of Streets with Dwellings" (12b). *Building a transformational movement is not only about prayer, church growth, evangelism and great conferences. From God's perspective, it is also about being compassionately present to heal the brokenhearted, feed the hungry, and set captives free from oppression.* Let's carefully guard against a view of awakening that is romanticized and over-spiritualized. In most cases, it comes down to the plain hard work of incarnating Jesus' love--giving a drink of water in his name without a thought of getting anything in return.

Renouncing Injustice

At the completion of the wall, the Israelites enjoyed an unprecedented week long celebration of the Feast of Tabernacles. The people came before the Lord to openly confess their sins, and the sins of their fathers. Ezra 9 and Nehemiah 9 show us clearly that the leaders and the people openly exposed significant and long standing "stronghold issues." The authenticity of what happened in the spirit was immediately evident in the natural. The people were ready to make right their moral wrongs and compromises. They had already renounced the practices of usury and economic servitude. Now they committed to forbid their daughters to intermarry with men of the local, foreign culture (10:30). They committed themselves to not buy or sell on the Sabbath, and to financially support the ministry of the temple. The bottom line: an oath of obedience, "We will not neglect the house of our God" (10:39). For them, this meant getting their hearts right with God, and having the courage to step up and stand out in contrast to the surrounding culture. Are we not responsible to confront deeply embedded, systemic sin resident in our culture, our cities, such as greed and racism? Are we not responsible to uphold a biblical definition of marriage: one man, one woman, for life?

In today's global village, the remnant, the "temple of the living God," holds the only real hope for serving as "repairer of broken walls, restorer of streets with dwellings." And this is not the work of pie-in-the-sky prayer meetings or "bless me" worship gatherings. No, it is laboring together at the broken places on the wall: returning to righteousness, embracing a lifestyle of brokenness and repentance, renouncing and reversing social injustice. This is still a relevant "blueprint" for the house of the Lord in our day. Honestly, it seems to me the prophetic voice of the remnant has turned pathetic. God help us to keep standing up and speaking up.

What are we Looking for?

If we're serious about opening the gates of our cities to spiritual awakening, we have to be ready to separate ourselves from the corruptions of our culture and put kingdom values on display. Let's glean all we can from this old covenant model. As new covenant Christians, with the covering of the blood of Jesus, his personal intercession on our behalf, and the power of his indwelling Spirit, we have the resources to release resurrection power into the darkest corners of our communities. What then can we learn and apply here? God's favor and blessing are released when we get to the real core of our spiritual compromises, confess them, and resolve to walk in the truth. **The more I meditate on Nehemiah, the more I get blessed seeing the tangible results of authentic spiritual reformation. I find these following outcomes astounding!**

- **At the dedication of the wall, the Levites were "sought out from where they lived" to come and lead worship. People went looking for the worship leaders to bring them into God's presence! (12:27).**

- **The joy of their celebration was so exuberant, they could be "heard far away" (12:43). Heartfelt appreciation and praise erupted in response to the goodness of the Lord. It appears their joy was uninhibited, loud, and noticeable.**

- **The people were "pleased with the ministering priests and Levites" (12:44b). The people of**

Judah were verbally and visibly supportive of their leaders, and it showed in their actions.

- All Israel "contributed the daily portions" to support the temple workers (12:47). People opened their purses to give first fruits and extra offerings to the work of the kingdom.

Bottom line, when people freely give of their time, money and energy above and beyond expectation, something untypical is going on. Returning from bondage in Babylon, these exiles were broken and humbled. In his graciousness, Yahweh opened the door for their return. He raised up gifted leaders—secular politicians, skilled laborers, prophets, priests, worship leaders—and called Israel back, not so much to a place, but to himself, the only true source of peace and spiritual prosperity. Clearly, this is one of the high water marks in all of Old Testament history.

So, what might this look like for us today? When we see people in our congregations supporting leadership, showing up for worship and prayer gatherings, making their time and energy available to serve, and joyously offering finances, we'll know something authentic is underway. And when leaders and laity in healthy congregations catch sight of the biblical blueprint for building a citywide church, we can begin touching new places of grace. In an increasing number of locales, I believe we are poised today to hear God's call and to prepare places for sustainable habitation in this 21st century of church history. As this drama unfolds, it will indeed be "his story."

Dr. Brad Greene, an engineer by training, was commissioned to do an exegetical study of Nehemiah in the context of the city movement in Knoxville, TN. His burden was to see the "Nehemiah Element" awakened in his city, but he noted a problem: "The Ezra Element (the Church) is trying to awaken Nehemiah, but Ezra does not have the influence or credibility in those contexts to awaken Nehemiah from his slumber. We believe it will take Nehemiah to awaken Nehemiah."[2] Currently, worldwide, the Spirit of God is awakening and calling forth the Nehemiahs to step out, assess the damage in their city, seek solutions and mobilize resources to repair broken walls and burned gates.

"See, I am Doing a New Thing"

I close with a prophetic word from the Lord delivered to Israel in a season of transition. I believe this is a "now word" for us today: *"Forget the former things; do not dwell on the past. See, I am doing a new thing! Now it springs up; do you not perceive it?" (Is 43:18, 19).* I'm encouraged. *"It's happening!"* The Body of Christ is *transitioning* from a focus on individual congregations, organizations and denominations towards a wider, inclusive understanding of the kingdom of God. That said, I want to make it clear here, and will say this again in Chapter 3, the identity and individual mandate of the local congregation is not going away! To me, the New Testament is clear: One church (in a city or region), comprised of a multiplicity of life-giving congregations, each with its own unique gifts, callings and distinctives. This will likewise remain true of denominations: theological convictions and distinctions will be with us until we sit at Jesus' feet in the New Jerusalem! *This is a "win-win-win," strong individual local churches, strong theological fellowships and streams, and a strong, cohesive citywide Body of Christ serving and blessing the city.*

This revelation is also *accelerating.* More are grasping the kingdom principles gleaned from Ezra, Haggai and Nehemiah, and discovering what "the house of the Lord" and "walls and gates" might look like in the twenty-first century context. *What a time to be alive and alert to this fresh work of the Spirit of God, bringing forth concrete answers to Jesus' prayer, that his followers would be "one, so that the world will believe."* Before we plunge into the practicalities of growing a city movement, I want to engage head-on the legitimacy of what is generally referred to as the "city church."

Chapter Three

"City Church:" Biblical? Achievable?

"Where do you get this idea that all of the churches across our community are to join some kind of 'city church?'" Whether I get this push back directly and verbally, or by overt non-participation, there are a lot of pastors and leaders of non-profits in our cities just not buying into this message and movement. I've already laid out a Prologue and two Chapters celebrating what I see as a timely work of God's Spirit to bring on-line concrete answers to Jesus' prayer for unity among his followers. But let's get real, there's resistance to this.

Is a citywide expression of Jesus' Body a biblical pattern? If so, what would it functionally look like in the context of a community comprised of a variety of churches, non-profit Christian organizations and a host of ethnic and Christian economic sub-cultures? Patch in the presence of Catholic churches, mainline Protestant Churches ("liberal" as distinct from "evangelical"), and Orthodox congregations, and the question gets even more complex. Historically, Catholic dogma holds that they are the only "true" church, tracing unbroken succession from the Apostle Peter. That's a big deal. The Orthodox streams stake a similar claim. Then enter the Protestant Reformation, with its four hundred years of exponential ecclesiastical fragmentation that has resulted in virtually tens of thousands of denominations. Protestants tend to stake claims to the legitimacy and autonomy of *their* denomination or congregation. But let's recognize also that there has been an increase of "para-church" endeavors pursuing their passion/mission through ministries parallel to the "church."

So, what does "one church, many congregations" realistically look like in a community? This is a fair question that calls for some compelling answers. We need to gain a realistic understanding of how a healthy, functional local church body participates in the wider Body. This is neither conformity, nor uniformity. But, as these citywide expressions are emerging across the world at present, this is the beauty of a unity found in diversity, and grown through maturity of character and an irenic spirit.

Generally, we can say the "Church" takes three expressions in our world. 1) **The Church universal**, all who have genuinely received God's grace gift of forgiveness and life in Jesus, and are sealed by the Holy Spirit, regardless of any formal church affiliation, Catholic, Orthodox or Protestant. The Father knows those who are truly his. 2) **The Church local,** individual congregations or house fellowships where there is a clear appointing of spiritual leadership that teaches, disciples, admonishes and disciplines its members. 3) **The "city church,"** a wider, inclusive expression of the Body of Christ in a city or region. Now, I doubt anyone would argue against the first two expressions above. But there are significant and legitimate questions about the legitimacy of calling the citywide expression of collective believers a "church." If you will stay with me on this, you will find that I prefer to call this expression a "kingdom community." No, such a citywide expression does not appoint elders. It does not have authority to discipline its members. It cannot and should not ask for a tithe from its participants. The local congregation is clearly God's vehicle for winning, growing and discipling followers of Jesus.

So, what am I really talking about here? I am talking about a diversity of born-again living stones from a variety of congregations identifying as a wider community committed to advancing God's kingdom, convinced that at some level, and in some endeavors, we are "better together." In light of my content in Chapter 1, to coin the title of a pop song from the 1970's, "We are Family." This is about a Father wanting to be with all of his kids, and wanting his kids to get along. This is about a Southern Baptist coming to appreciate and pray with an Assembly of God, an Hispanic worshiping alongside an African-American, a millennial and a boomer working together to mentor at-risk kids. *Whatever congregation or affiliation you identify with, can we not all embrace the call "to reach the whole city with the whole gospel through the whole church?" The common, cohesive mission of the "city church" is to work cooperatively and collaboratively to win and disciple the collective souls of a city.* I believe deeply we can steward a sustainable culture committed to praying, caring for the needy and sharing the gospel with the lost. Jesus, our Chief Shepherd, calls all of us in any given community to serve as "under-shepherds," working towards the same goal of serving the least and saving the lost.

One of my favorite author is Philip Yancey. I love this brother's honesty, and superb word-crafting. I want to quote him at length here, as his words so powerfully confirm my point:

> Diversity complicates rather than simplifies life. Perhaps for this reason we tend to surround ourselves with people of similar age, economic class, and opinion. Church offers a place where infants and grandparents, unemployed and executives, immigrants and blue bloods can come together. Just yesterday I sat sandwiched between an elderly man hooked up to a puffing oxygen tank and a breast feeding baby who grunted loudly and contentedly throughout the sermon. Where else can we go to find that mixture? In his great prayer in John 17, Jesus stressed one request above all others: "that they may be one." The existence of 38,000 denominations worldwide demonstrates how poorly we have fulfilled Jesus' request. I wonder how different the church would look to a watching world, not to mention how different history would look, if Christians were more deeply marked by love and unity." *Christianity Today*, Nov. 2008

So, do *you* wonder what the church might look like to the watching world in *your* community if there was a citywide expression of authentic John 17 community emerging and growing in your midst?

The Biblical Data

On the Mount of Olives, we see a rare, transparent look into Jesus' heart as he weeps over the city of Jerusalem, and its inhabitants. He had come first to his own people. He was soon to suffer and die as their Messiah. In light of our theme from Chapter 1, notice the familial language, "I have longed to gather your children together, as a hen gathers her chicks under her wings" (Lu. 13:34). This is a clear, consistent offer from the heart of the Father for nearness and nurture. But Jesus weeps, agonized by the response, "you were not willing" (Lu. 13:34). Clearly, the collective souls of Jerusalem carried a corporate identity and responsibility in their response to revelatory truth, and an offer of personal relationship to their Redeemer.

We see a further expression of Jesus' agony over the collective souls of a city recorded in Revelation, but this time with hope. But what is clear and compelling to me is this virtual "last word" of the New Testament canon, the personal words to real people in real cities brought through John the Apostle. I realize there are a variety of ways to interpret the letters to the seven churches Jesus dictates to John. But what is unmistakable to me is that Jesus brings a city-specific, contextual commendation and critique to his people dwelling in each of these seven cities. Of course in Ephesus, Smyrna and Philadelphia there were house churches all over town, "ekklesias" (called out ones), churches, congregations. But *Jesus clearly addresses the collective souls of the redeemed, the totality of saints living in that place, with a message tailored to its unique context and culture.*

It has become evident to me that in the First Century, the Lord dealt with his people on two levels, through "house churches," individual congregations with elder leadership, pastors and teachers, and also on this city level I am describing. The Book of Acts is replete with both. "Then *the church* throughout Judea, Galilee and Samaria enjoyed a time of peace. *It* was strengthened and encouraged by the Holy Spirit" (Acts 9:31, emphases mine). How can anyone get around the reality that herein is a description of the "regional," collective expression of Christ's Body, and that there is a distinctive, geographical work of the Spirit in that region? And this corporate, cohesive "family" experienced the common awe of God's attributes and character. They also witnessed a clear supernatural growth of the overall Body of Christ, which occurred in specific local assemblies. So, of course there were numerous individual congregations in that region. That's a given. So, it is appropriate to talk not "one or the other" but rather "both/and." And beginning with "the church" in Antioch, where the disciples were first called "Christians" (11:26), a new city-reaching strategy was birthed by the Holy Spirit, described in Acts 13:1-3. While "the church at Antioch" was worshiping the Lord and fasting, the Holy Spirit set Barnabas and Saul apart for a new work, and sent them out. Where? To specific cities, one after another.

It is not a surprise, then, to see how Paul addresses his letter to the Romans: "To all in Rome who are loved by God and called to be saints" (1:7). Likewise to Corinth, "To the church of God in Corinth, to those sanctified in Christ Jesus and called to be holy, together with all those everywhere who call on the name of the Lord Jesus Christ" (1:2). So, here it is, both the "city church" gathered at Corinth, and reference to the "church universal," in Paul's words, "all those everywhere." And we see the same "city church" address in Ephesians 1:1, Philippians 1:1, and Colossians 1:2. Look also at Paul's charge to Timothy: "The reason I left you in Crete was that you might straighten out what was left unfinished and *appoint elders in every town…*" (Tit. 1:5, emphasis mine).

So, we may ask, was this "city church" expression unique only to the emerging, first century church, an expression that preceded an increased organization of "local church" congregations? Did the "city church" have its day, to be super-ceded by a plethora of autonomous congregations, and endless denominations? While some may argue so, I personally think not. I come down squarely affirming the reality of all three expressions, the church universal, the church local and the church across a city or region. *I believe we are returning to a correct understanding and functioning of Jesus' Body on earth. I am convinced we are in a day when the Holy Spirit is initiating and igniting a restoration of the identity and responsibility of the Body of Christ in geographically specific communities to collaborate on the completion of Jesus' Great Commission to win and disciple all peoples.*

A Holy Temple Rising

I want now to turn to Apostles Paul and Peter to give us more light on what this "city church" expression might look like. In the New Covenant context, *the nexus of relationship is neither tent, tabernacle or the splendor of a temple. The nexus is the inner, spiritual chamber of any heart that makes a place for the presence of deity to dwell.* When any person hears the gospel and receives its benefit, he or she is "marked with a seal, the promised Holy Spirit, who is a deposit guaranteeing our inheritance" (Eph. 1:13, 14). Writing to the believers in Corinth, Paul posed this profound question: "Don't you know that you yourselves are God's temple and that God's Spirit lives in you?" (1 Cor. 3:16). This is true of any individual who receives the gift of forgiveness in Christ. Likewise, it is true of the larger corporate Body of believers: "For we are the temple of the living God. As God has said: 'I will live with them and walk among them, and I will be their God, and they will be my people" (2 Cor. 6:16). Paul is referencing the original revelation of God's heart from Leviticus 26 (Chapter 1). From Old Testament to New, there is constancy and constancy of his desire and design.

This amazing design, which frankly exceeds comprehension, is more vividly captured in the Hebraic language employed by both Paul and Peter. Having established God's purpose of removing the wall of separation/distinction between Jews and Gentiles, and creating "one new man," all believers now have one common "access" to God the Father (the "church universal," Eph. 2:14-18). As if this new reality is not profound enough, Paul goes on to describe the Body of Christ as "members of God's household," built on the truth and teachings of the apostles and prophets, with Jesus the "chief cornerstone." When we talk about a "city church" expression, it is imperative that any such movement in a city be built on the rock of revelatory truth given us through God's chosen apostles and prophets. So, what does a non-negotiable "cornerstone" of doctrinal truth look like?

I believe we must find unwavering agreement on at least three core points of orthodox doctrinal truth: 1) the triune nature of the Godhead, as revealed in Scripture, 2) Jesus Christ is Son of God and Son of Man, who alone offers the gift of salvation by grace, received through faith, and 3) the Scriptures are the Word of God that guides our lives. This immediately leaves out of a bona fide expression of "city church" any and all who "waffle" on these three touchstones. Thus, so-called "liberal" churches and cults will self-select out of any association that is anchored in the absolutes of a truly biblically based gospel.

Now, here's the high point of all architectural blueprints ever dreamed or designed in the history of humankind:

> *"In him (Christ) the whole building is joined together and rises to become a holy temple in the Lord. And in him you too are being built together to become a dwelling place in which God lives by his Spirit" (Eph. 2:21,22).*

Only the love and grace of Jesus can join together men and women, young and old, of diverse culture, color, and language into a singular spiritual society! And this holy endeavor is not static, but fluid. The word "rises" (present indicative tense) depicts an on-going process, literally, "is rising…and will continue to rise." The phrase "are being built" is likewise present indicative, literally "is growing." This living Body of Christ, present on earth, localized in language groups, cultures and communities, is "being built." And the ultimate goal is to become a "dwelling place" for our triune God. And

Paul is clear: this can only happen by the supernatural grace of the Holy Spirit selecting and putting each living stone in its place. Any localized expression of this living temple is thus a "work in progress," with living stones being added and cemented in, until the close of human history.

Let's be honest. This is Holy Scripture, the Word of God. But in view of the reality of any given real place in the real world, this language can sound hyper-spiritual. Where do we find any semblance of this in space/time reality? *With so much disagreement and incongruence over theology and ecclesiology, and so many members of Christ's Body relationally at odds, is Paul describing the same world you and I live in?*

Remember, we're not talking utopia here. We're talking about an achievable, "work-in-progress" foreshadowing a future, hoped-for reality. We're talking about the annual "Kingdom Come" gathering of saints in the sports arena in Kingston, Ontario, with the venue booked through 2015, and a vision to increase participation each year. We're talking about fourteen venues for the annual Global Day of Prayer in the Greater Toronto Area, each gathering distinguished by ethnic or linguistic expression, but all open to the wider Body of Christ. We're talking about Love and Care Ministries in Abilene, Texas, a citywide endeavor to meet the needs of the poor and marginalized. We're talking about the historic emergence of a greater Kansas City kingdom coalition, "Elevate K.C.," with an initial missional focus: "helping every urban elementary child read at grade level and, and expanding and serving youth summer learning programs." This endeavor is comprised of thirty five to forty leaders of major ministry networks and marketplace initiatives. Visible, viable snapshots of a "holy temple rising" in real places. No, this is not a hyper-spiritual fantasy, but achievable when Jesus' followers in any place embrace the benefits of his John 17 priestly prayer.

Peter, a Jew familiar with Old Covenant language and imagery, brings added light to Paul's revelation of God's "desire and design to dwell." In 1 Peter, chapter 2, he begins with a straight-up exhortation to his readers to get rid of all the salacious, insidious attitudes that cause suspicion and separation among fellow believers. Then, depicting Jesus as "the living Stone—rejected by men but chosen by God" (1 Pe. 2:4), he says of his readers—

> "...you also, like living stones, are being built into a spiritual house to be a holy priesthood, offering spiritual sacrifices acceptable to God through Jesus Christ" (1 Pe. 2:5)

Literally, the meaning here is "lively stones." The connotation is sprightly, spontaneous, vibrant! The makings of this "house" are living, organic materials! Now, Old Covenant Jews prided themselves on the beauty and majesty of their Temple. But the New Covenant, and with it a new dispensation of grace, offers a living temple of incomparable beauty, a unity of life comprised of a diversity of living, vibrant building blocks.

So, in any given place, this could look like a squarish Southern Baptist stone, with a roundish, asymmetrical Pentecostal stone overhead. And to the left, a born-again Episcopalian stone, with purple, liturgical hue, and to the right, a perfect spot and fit for a born-again black Nigerian tribal chief. And what holds such diversity together? What minimizes friction between the stones? The soft, pliable cement, the agape love of Jesus, the God-given capacity to honor and prefer others above ourselves. Clearly, under the inspiration of the Holy Spirit, the two Apostles are here offering Old Covenant Jews consolation over the soon-to-come loss of their Temple, and inspiration to Gentile believers, who never even set foot in the Jewish structure, but now have embraced the mystery and marvel of being the very locus of God's presence!

And all stones, corporately, comprise a "holy (royal) priesthood." Every believer is a priest, with the privilege of honoring and serving the one High Priest. And the "spiritual sacrifices" offered are those of the heart: adoration, praise, honor, and service to the Redeemer, who already offered the once-for-all sacrifice for all humankind. So, *the people of God, restored in his image, bear both the sanctity of priests, and the dignity of kings.* And, for a twofold purpose: 1) to "declare the praises of him who called you out of darkness, and 2) to "live good lives among the pagans," so that even if they scorn you, they will "see your good deeds" and give honor and glory to God. *In short, this living, organic household of faith, cemented together by the love of Christ, in any given city, region or nation, is to engage in proclamation of forgiveness to those still lost, and demonstration of Jesus' compassion to those in need—sharing the good news and demonstrating love through good works.*

In Chapters 4 and 5, I will get "boots-on-the-ground" practical about what this "royal priesthood" might look like in your city. But I need to be clear. Not everyone is going to readily agree with signing on to participate in this "city church." Here's some advice. Don't get annoyed or irritated with those who don't quickly sign on to this vision, just keep loving and blessing them. The reality is, you need to acknowledge the right of the pastors, elders and deacons of local congregations to differ with you, hold back or self-select out of the mix of the citywide Body. Major on relational/organic submission to the Lordship of Jesus, and minor on organizational structure. Renounce a spirit of promotion, and pronounce on-going invitation to the Spirit to stir and bring others in.

You will find, in time, as the health of Jesus' Body across the city grows, and the stories of changed lives increase, some of those who have had reservations might start dropping in, one at a time. I have found that some leaders sign on slowly, choosing to participate in small ways. Accept them where they are. Appreciate their contribution. Welcome them into the "family," and bless them in the spirit of John 17.

Mystery Made Known

I want to elucidate another piece in Ephesians, one of those Pauline nuggets that provokes deep reflection:

> *"His intent was that now, through the church, the manifold wisdom of God should be made known to the rulers and authorities in the heavenly realms…"* (Eph. 3:10)

The "wisdom of God," tracing back to Ephesians 2, is the plan to provide his own Son as an atoning sacrifice, to remove the barrier between man and God, and between man and man. Thus, Christ's blood "destroyed the barrier" between Jew and Gentile, man and woman, rich and poor, powerful and powerless, making "one new man" in Jesus Christ. This wisdom, says Paul, is "manifold." So, what does *this* mean? Literally, multi-faceted, multi-colored. The plan of the Father to reverse the curses of Satan and sin were laid out from the beginning of creation, as the fall of man came as no surprise to a sovereign God. This implies a panoramic view, inclusive of a variety of aspects and phases (e.g., settling on the plan, selection of the promised seed, prophecies pointing towards the coming hope, the incarnation, atoning sacrifice, resurrection, and the power of the indwelling Holy Spirit to sanctify and empower). The language here describes something multi-dimensional and magnificent, like an ever-changing, awe-inspiring sunset over a lake, ocean or mountain.

And consider this implication from the text. Angels and demons have been watching this "wisdom" unfold over eons of time, intrigued as to how holy God would repair this breech. And here, in Jesus, the promised one, the plan is put in place! And it worked! *And so, when believers, as living stones, honor and prefer one another, walk in love and work together, this is a demonstration in space-time reality that the redemptive plan of God has succeeded.* The Body of Jesus Christ works! For sure Christians are not yet perfect. We are a people in process. But God's unmerited grace, displayed through the Cross, cements the diversity of saints together as a witness of supernatural oneness. And when radically different living stones are cemented together in Jesus love, there is a beam of light displayed to the whole creation—human, angelic, demonic—that this wisdom was supreme, and the plan works.

Let me share a living illustration. Siliguri, in North India, is a nexus for a variety of cultures, language groups and religions, in close proximity to Nepal, Bhutan, and Bangladesh. Just being in this place, one is bombarded with the sounds, sights and smells of Hinduism, Buddhism, Islam, and a host of other syncretistic religious expressions. But beginning with a Prayer Summit in 2005, key leaders in the Body of Christ came to a holy resolve: to sow their lives into Jesus' prayer for unity in John 17:21-23, to pray together every Saturday morning, for one another and for the kingdom of God to increase in their city. They engage in collaborative outreach into other cities in North India, and into neighboring nations, distributing clothing, food and medicines to the needy, and sharing the gospel. I have been privileged to walk alongside three point leaders for this movement, Joshua, Daniel and Enos. In October, 2011, I inquired, "Joshua, bring me up to date on what you're doing." Churches had just joined resources to put on an appreciation dinner for the mostly Hindu government officials of Siliguri, a tangible witness of oneness. Appreciating this effort, the Mayor gave Joshua opportunity to preach. *An authentic, tangible demonstration of the love of Christ followers, serving a city, is compellingly attractive.* And, in light of Paul's word in Ephesians 3:10, this oneness overflows out and up even into heavenly places, like an illuminated billboard or beacon light that advertises an attractive product. The gospel of love, humility and sacrificial service are the strongest weapons we have to expose and overcome the long-held lies and deceptions of the powers of hell.

So, I just returned from Prayer Summit number nine in Siliguri (June, 2013). Here's a rather astounding update. Numerous times over the years, in my Western, linear thinking, I've tried to encourage these dear brothers to create a formal citywide leadership team, with monthly meetings, goals and assignments. Well, they just didn't do it "my way." Instead, while worshiping the Lord and praying for Siliguri and her peoples every Saturday, the Holy Spirit has faithfully stirred them with vision, consensus to collaboratively advance the gospel. The results of this approach are nothing less than extraordinary! In October, 2012, numerous congregations came together for a three night tent crusade. Typically, gatherings like this demand the presence of security guards. Not one was employed, and not one disturbance occurred. On the final night, around twenty thousand attended, with an estimate of four to five hundred finding Christ. They're doing this again in October, 2013.

Three particular people groups have been historically resistant to the gospel: Biharis, West Bengalis and Muslims. Suddenly, spontaneously, all three are responding to the gospel and are showing up in local churches. One Bihari teen-age girl brought eighty to ninety peers to a Young Life meeting recently. Churches and ministries are now partnering and sharing resources to reach prostitutes and their children in the red light district, and assist in the development of sustainable livelihood. This past Christmas, the city government approached these brothers, asking them to organize a public presentation in the new downtown commercial center, "In the Name of Christmas," with Christmas songs, dancing and preaching. And the government paid them ten thousand rupees to cover set-up charges!

So if this isn't exciting enough, here's the "big one!" (the Ephesians 3:10 beam of light into the heavenlies). Every year, most Indian cities host a Puja Festival to honor local and national gods and goddesses. In Siliguri, the Puja Committee had done this for the past ninety-nine years. Well, this past year they compared notes, and determined that the Festival was costing a lot of money, provoked social violence, and "wasn't really doing anyone any good." So, they disbanded their committee, cancelled Puja altogether, and gave a large stage and props to the Churches to put on a worship celebration!

This, would you not agree, is authentic, biblical "city transformation?" Not by might, human wisdom or well developed organization, but by the leading and creative empowerment of God's Spirit. And not only transformation, but replication, is already underway. These brothers and others have already catalyzed John 17 prayer groups in the neighboring cities of Kurseong and Mirik, and have a bold vision of the sovereign Spirit stirring a movement in the whole region. And when the Lord is on the move like this, be careful to curb human enthusiasm. Don't start running out ahead of Him. Keep discerning his prompts, learning his ways and following his lead. Keep Jesus' words ever in view, "I will build my church…"

Compelling Reasons to Build Unity in a City Context

If a story like this doesn't grab your attention, let me add a few points. You may still be wrestling with this idea of the "city church." Or, if not, you likely know someone who is, and a few more compelling arguments may prove helpful. I'd like to suggest some reasons for kingdom leaders to invest more in building John 17:21-23 unity. Having been involved over three decades helping birth and build the citywide church, in many communities, in many nations, I want to build a case for getting involved in promoting such a covenant community in your city.

So, why invest time, energy and resources in building the "city church?"

1. **It's biblical.** Unity in diversity is a reflection of the Trinity itself, three separate persons operating with three distinct functions, identifying as one person. Jesus specifically prayed that the relationship between his followers would reflect the nature of his relationship with the Father and the Spirit.

2. **There is inherent value in collegial relationships.** In Paul's words, we are to be "like-minded, having the same love, being one in spirit and purpose" (Phil. 2:2). Also, he commends the saints in Thessalonica for the authenticity of their love for one another. In city after city, over twenty years, I have observed kingdom colleagues--mixed gender, multi-generational, ethnically diverse—spending

time together, enjoying one another, laughing and jesting, bearing one another's burdens, crying and praying for each other. I know men and women, leaders in cities so deeply bonded, they would be willing to die for one another. Isn't this what Jesus modeled, and commended to his followers? Having friends like this is a rare treasure.

3. **The Body's witness of oneness has an apologetic power** ("one…that the world will believe," Jo. 17:23). When we get along, and serve together in the trenches of our cities, our humility, our love for one another, is noticeably attractive. Instead of seeing fragmented, disjointed "body parts," a community sees firsthand that "Christianity actually works."

4. **We share the privilege of united intercession for the outpouring of the Spirit with signs, wonders and conversions** (Acts 4:29-31). When saints gather across dividing lines of different theologies and ecclesiologies, to pray for the needs of a city, God gives favor. Paul urges, "first of all," that the Church prays for government officials, so there can be an environment conducive for the sharing of the gospel (1 Ti. 2:1-6). You can build a culture of intercessory investment, praying into a preferred future for your city, with watchful expectation of return on the investment.

5. **It is good wisdom and stewardship to coordinate serving ministries;** this is the answer to the proverbial question, "Why re-invent the wheel?" Increasingly, we are seeing models of church and non-profit organizations sharing office space, personnel and resources. Serving ministries can increasingly communicate and coordinate to avoid duplication and competition. Of course there will always be a plethora of different passions and missional endeavors in play in any given venue. But to see ourselves functionally on the same team is wise stewardship, and can only maximize further extension of kingdom influence.

6. **To share together a corporate responsibility to win and disciple the collective souls in the city.** It is healthy to understand that we are not competing for the same "market share" of souls, but as "under-shepherds" serving the Good Shepherd of all souls, we ask God to prosper one another's outreach endeavors, and rejoice together when new names are written in the book of life.

7. **Maximize training and equipping opportunities** (Eph. 4:11). This is a huge benefit for a local Body of Christ. In my city, we offer the Perspectives Course annually, hosted by a local congregation, but available to anyone in the city. Recently, a local church hosted "Jesus in the Koran," training Christians how to reach out to Muslims, another congregation hosts "Jubilee" annually, a women's

conference, and invites citywide participation. In the Spring of 2012, a group of Christian Education Directors joined in with the international "4/14" movement (a worldwide stirring of prayer among children), and put a program together on a Saturday. In the Fall of 2012, the Kingston Transformation Network hosted citywide the "Love and Respect" conference, aimed at strengthening marriages and families.

8. **Release the synergy of combined gifts and callings,** empowered by the Holy Spirit. Going forward from here, I believe Christ's Body, across a city or region, is to move towards more of a functional unity, all parts, callings and gifts at work according to the revelation of Ephesians 4:1-16, where the whole Body "builds itself up in love, as each part does its work." *Is this unity and synergy meant only for one congregation, or organization? No, this is meant for a healthy Body—living stones cemented to other living stones—fitted together in a city or region, every part helping every other part.* As the variety of kingdom assets come into right alignment with one another, we get "synergy." One plus one no longer equals just two, but three. And three plus three equals nine. Exponential increase of energy, released through the synergy of collaboration.

As you process these points, you may already be "on the same paradigm page" with me, and I'm just preaching to the choir. Or, you may be reflecting on this rationale and find yourself thinking, "This is a high bar--nowhere close to the reality of how the Body of Christ relates in *my city.*" This may be true, and disappointing. But remember that in any new movement there are always innovators and early adopters. Some courageous pioneer needs to start *somewhere.* Just keep the door of your heart open for new friends to show up, one by one, and keep sharing your vision for the "witness of oneness" of the Body of Christ in your city. And warmly welcome the "fence sitters" and late adopters when they decide to show up and plug in.

Now, I invite you to slip on a hard hat, grab your tool-belt, put on your boots and head with me to the construction site.

Chapter Four

Leadership Wineskins For City and Regional Movements

Here is a core question I've carried in my soul for many years:

> *How does a united, praying Body of Christ in a city strengthen relationships and partnerships between its diversity of kingdom assets (pastors, non-profit and marketplace leaders, compassion ministries, intercessors) to labor together to bring more people into God's kingdom and minister to the needs of the poor and marginalized?*

We are seeing a virtual explosion of creative and contextual answers to this question. Here's the heart of the matter: God is aligning his people in specific places to walk in covenantal love, engage in transformational prayer and partner in collaborative endeavors that serve the least and offer redemption to the spiritually lost. Bottom line: we are in a season where a holistic paradigm of transformational change is emerging. This development involves *a variety and synergy of approaches to transformational change, informed by Scripture, guided by the Holy Spirit and implemented in communities by men and women of faith and perseverance. In short, "new wineskins of kingdom community"* (see "A Sampling of City Transformation Strategies," Appendix).

For these new wineskins to work and be fruitful, the full array of spiritual leadership gifts and callings are required. From 1999 to 2011 I was privileged to serve as one of four Conveners of the National City Impact Roundtable, an association of veteran and emerging city-reaching practitioners. At our annual CIR in Cedar Rapids, IA, in 2005, we invited some "city stories." Steve Capper, one of the principal leaders of Mission Houston, brought a timely word: "If your movement is going to grow and develop to the next level, someone has to wake up every morning thinking about the city." While this sounds like common sense, a "no brainer," what Steve shared is not to be taken for granted. *In my view, as a veteran coach, cities that get traction and accelerate towards the next level of development have at point a called, competent leader or core of leaders who wake up every morning thinking and praying, "Lord, where are you moving in our city, and how can we join you?"*

In my opinion, the key component most essential for shaping a new wineskin for the Body of Christ in a city are leaders uniquely prepared and appointed by God to call together a team with citywide vision. Of course there may be a small core of like-minded leaders sick of status quo, and hungry to go somewhere fresh. But typically, there is a person or persons with a mantle, beaming with vision and bursting with passion to press into the new thing the Holy Spirit is doing.

Here's my take on current reality. While biblical principles are common, there are a variety of applications of those principles on the ground, each with its own cultural nuances and footprint. What we're really after is the synergistic balancing of the best of natural human talent and innovation with the blessing of supernatural anointing. We must continually guard against our propensity to organize, monetize and franchise these endeavors. But the real key, in every kingdom experiment, is keeping Jesus' great commandments and priestly prayer at the core of who we are, and all we do.

Leadership is the Key

One aspect of my calling is to allow the Lord to use me trans-locally, helping birth and develop new expressions of kingdom community. Frankly, I'm humbled by this, as I often feel challenged by most of the situations I work with.

In May 2007, I received an email from Bryan, an American tent-maker living in Skopje, Macedonia. The leaders there had begun holding Leaders Prayer Summits in 2002. Sensing God was up to something fresh, they weren't getting clear direction on where to go next. A friend of Bryan's knew of me, and recommended my original book, *Citywide Prayer Movements*. Bryan sent an email, "I've just read your book. It seems like you may be able to help us here in Skopje move to the next level." So, we all know of Paul's "Macedonian call." This was mine! Reading Bryan's e-mail, what I heard in the Spirit, was, "Can you come over and help us?"

And so, in October, 2007, I facilitated a Prayer Summit for Skopje kingdom leaders, and a few from other cities in Macedonia. The Lord was powerfully present. He is so gracious to always come when we open the door. Earlier, I had arranged to meet with a core group of key leaders following the Summit. So here I sat, with my associate Glen Weber, a pastor from Pasadena, at the end of a long conference table. We de-briefed the Summit, and began talking generally about next steps for the city movement. Then the "nudge" from the Spirit. "You're on, now. Do your job!"

I shared that in order for them to move forward and develop their movement to the next level, they needed to select and put in place a team of servant leaders who would steward a sustainable expression of covenant relationships among the leaders and congregations of Skopje. Typically, I explained, this involved regular corporate prayer and missional endeavors of some kind in the city. In my spirit, I could hear a collective "gulp" (in Macedonian, of course!). I also picked up some normal, cross-cultural resistance. "Who is this guy, telling us what to do?" Frankly, in my humanity, I was asking the same questions!

We floundered around awhile with some further conversation. I heard the Lord say again, "Do your job. Get this done!" At junctures like this, it is imperative to hear the Lord clearly. If I miss this, and mix in my own agenda or desired outcome, I can mess things up badly. It is hard enough doing this in one's own culture, where you know the nuances. But in another culture, the learning curve is steep.

So, I explained: "Friends, you invited me here, I'm a guest in your country and culture. But I believe I've been sent from the Lord in season to help you move forward. What we are talking about here is above and beyond the distinctions of human culture. This is about the Lord and Head of the Church of Skopje wanting to advance the expression of his kingdom in your city and nation. I would be failing in my assignment if we do not put a servant leadership team in place here today."

After some healthy discussion, there was a softening of resistance, and a consensus to proceed. With the amazing, gentle guidance of the Spirit, utilizing a selection process I have used numerous times, they selected an initial group of servant leaders, the Skopje City Church Leadership Team. As we parted that afternoon, I recall warning the team that the enemy would likely resist this bold step. I didn't want to sound negative, but obediently delivered the caution. Indeed, within weeks, they found themselves working through a trial, some dissension from within, and some skepticism and criticism from without. After weathering warfare reminiscent of Nehemiah 4, they have been up and running and growing ever since. The team is fluid. Over four years, some have slipped out, others stepped up. In October, 2011, after a four year investment, my formal coaching role was completed. I continue a personal friendship and consulting role with the point man of the Skopje movement.

In Kingston, Canada, in February of 2007, I facilitated the most dramatic shift of city leadership paradigms I've ever been a part of. I was wrapping up a Prayer Summit, and pitched some ideas for a new leadership structure I was envisioning for city movements. Around fifteen of the core leaders lingered. I had made a rough graphic of what this looked like, a smudged, crinkly overhead transparency, my very first shot envisioning Peter's picture of the "royal priesthood" I introduced to you in the Prologue, a diverse remnant of leaders representing the Body of Christ. I finished my "pitch," then asked, "What do you think?"

I was stunned. Roger, a local business owner and intercessor, spoke up straightway: "Well, okay, let's do this!" As in, let's put this model in place *now, here*. Well, everyone knew that the two principal leaders of the existing Kingston Pastors Prayer Fellowship were in the room. I sensitively stepped out, and explained the simple process I had developed for selecting servant leaders to put this wineskin in place. Everyone was thumbs up. By secret ballot, they selected five individuals, and then indicated that they wanted Roger to serve at point. Now, this all may seem fresh and innovative. But it was also awkward, because neither of the two existing leaders were selected. We gathered the five into the middle, prayed over them, and the "Kingston Transformation Network" was birthed in a heartbeat.

Sure, there were hurt feelings. But the two former leaders had grace to maturely step back and allow this "new thing" to come forth. And yes it was a challenging first year shaping and filling this new wineskin. But as diplomatic and sensitive as we must be navigating these transitions, *this process must be less about human feelings and insecurity, and more about the desire and design of the Lord to display his glory on our cities.* Sometimes old things, right for their season, must die, to make room for fresh ideas and leaders skilled to implement them.

In it for the Long Haul

I'm a long hauler. I want to see the labors in my own city, and in other cities I coach, sustained over time. Thus, I love the idea best captured by the title of a book by Eugene Peterson, *A Long Obedience in the Same Direction.* Remember, in our Old Testament time line, the process of restoring the physical temple and the centrality of worship, confession, and social justice, occurred over the span of some ninety years, involving a variety of phases, personnel, and problem-solving. As I write, I'm engaged in numerous venues helping to facilitate the passing of the baton of stewardship of the city wineskin off to younger, emerging leaders. They have different language, fresh ideas and a different pace. But I'm finding they share the same core passion to advance God's kingdom. This multi-generational partnering leadership is imperative if we hope to see our endeavors bring measurable change to our culture over time.

Let me be clear on what we're talking about by sharing an historical example. John and Charles Wesley, with their band of "Methodists" in eighteenth century England, model this kind of leadership with a long view. They were available to God for a reformation of spiritual life that resulted in conversions, radical holiness, and social change. Historians agree that the spiritual awakening through the Wesleys and George Whitefield was critical in sparing England from a devastating equivalent of the French Revolution. The Wesley brothers provided a minimal organizational structure that maximized a work of the Holy Spirit, forming "classes" and "bands" to sustain what God had initiated. The movement was marked by a balance of spiritual piety and biblical justice. Without necessarily duplicating the same structures today, we would be wise to discern and implement organizational models that are effective for giving both depth and breadth to a reformational work of the Holy Spirit.

Giving Leadership to the City-Wide Church

Let's explore more concretely what a city transformational movement looks like in current reality. *How does one church, expressed through a diversity of congregations, really work?* There are a variety of contextual adaptations on the landscape. Our heavenly Father does not "move" a standardized product, like vitamins or kitchenware. He does not crank out city movements with a cookie-cutter. If we truly get the spirit of this right, the substance and structure can take a variety of forms. If you are reading this, and find yourself in a preliminary stage of envisioning a new kingdom wineskin in your city or region, consider the following steps that might help to get you up and running.

Catalyzing a Movement: Helpful Components

From my experience, the following components depict some common ways in which the Holy Spirit is working to catalyze transformational city movements that are sustained over time. These components are surely not intended to be sequential or comprehensive. If you've read my Prologue and first three Chapters, you already know that my own story is strongly weighted towards building relationships of deep trust, cultivating a culture of corporate prayer, out of which flows a commonly shared consensus to engage missional endeavors. In other contexts, the beginning of a movement may be catalyzed by an event that pulls Christians together, a crisis in your community, or a glaring societal need that compels kingdom leaders to act. In the Royal Priesthood matrix I have been using, there are two broad, distinct sides to the leadership roundtable, the Church component ("Ezra"), and the vocational/cultural component ("Nehemiah"). Here's another helpful input from Brad Greene:

> "It is our recommendation that a comprehensive model for city transformation should include a neutral convener focusing on the resources of the city-at-large, and another focusing on the resources of the Church in the City." [1]

In my view, the "champion" neutral leaders in both Church and marketplace spheres may function in two parallel leadership teams. That model will take a significant measure of communication and coordination. But my preference, in the Lord's grace and leading, would have the two function together on one citywide team, as my Royal Priesthood model indicates. Here's a sampling of components that can serve to catalyze increased kingdom activity across a community:

1. **Hear and heed what the Holy Spirit is saying to the Church.** In your personal times with the Lord, small group prayer and conversation

with colleagues, or corporate gatherings, listen carefully for what is on God's heart for his Church. Listen for stories coming from other cities and regions. Listen for cues from culture shapers, men and women of influence *(To Transform a City, Swanson and Williams, Good Cities, Barth, Center Church,* Keller, *Why Cities Matter,* Um & Buzzard). Tune into what the Lord is saying and doing in local prayer meetings or conversations. Bringing forth a new wineskin calls for courage to step outside the status quo, heed God's voice and lead others in a new direction. Fresh vision may come through reading a book, or exploring a website (www.cityreaching.com, www.gospelmovements.com). I would commend one excellent, timeless message (Tim Keller's closing plenary, Movement Day 2012, available at www.movementday.com). Here's my premise: if the Spirit of God is truly at work bringing John 17 communities on-line, and wants one to emerge in your "backyard," *he will be speaking, and give grace for someone to be hearing!*

2. **Pray earnestly for God to ignite a movement of prayer in your city or area.** Typically, he stirs pioneer leaders and intercessors in a local setting to call the Body to return to Christ as first love, repent of sinful compromises, and hunger for spiritual awakening. Take heed to the Lord's "If... then" promise of 2 Chronicles 7:14. Always, it seems, in every city, men and women have labored in secret, in their "closets," wrestling with God and

persevering in prayer for this to happen. Make an effort to find the Isaiah 62 "watchmen on the walls" in your area, mature intercessors who have been praying into a vision like this for years, perhaps decades. Leaders follow other strong leaders. And leaders tend to trust leaders they know to be anchored with a deep prayer life. Thus, a single leader who is hearing God clearly, and praying in agreement with his will, or a small cadre of like-minded men and women, can catalyze other colleagues to go deeper seeking the Lord for their community.

3. **Increase a call to unity among the leaders in your city.** Set aside extended periods to seek the Lord (Ps 27:4, 8), "dwell together" (Ps 133:1), and build organic, heart-to-heart unity from the inside out. This could be a Leadership Prayer Encounter, a retreat, or a "day away." However you format this, or whatever you call it, it is important to "get out of Dodge," downshift the gears of busy-ness, and spend time sitting together at the Lord's feet. Often, it is advisable to invite an outside facilitator to lead this. Cultivate a covenantal commitment to model the unity of Christ's Body (Eph 4:1-6; Jn 17:21-23). Begin asking the Lord to stir fresh vision and strategy for more effectively reaching the community.

4. **Identify and empower servant leaders to guide the emerging movement.** These individuals,

typically a mix of pastors and non-profit leaders, are responsible to define and broaden the movement. They are to model mutual submission, honoring one another in humility. They seek consensus for advancing the vision for a citywide movement. In many cases, making the transition from old paradigm structures (e.g., ministerial lunches, pastors prayer fellowships, a business leaders breakfast, etc.) to a new one will be awkward. If they don't say it, other leaders will think it, "Who are *you* to change what we've been doing, who are *you* to lead?" In many cities, I have encouraged the formation of an "Interim Envisioning Team" to provide leadership for these early transitions. This team is fluid, leading from the grass roots up, not top down. Also, it is helpful having an experienced city-reaching coach assist in the formation and development of this team.

5. **Engage a Nehemiah-like assessment of the broken walls and burned gates of your city.** This is the most attractive and compelling component for marketplace leaders. Put an earnest inquiry before the Lord, "Where is the pain and brokenness in our city that you are wanting to touch?" Many leaders go straight to the Mayor, City Manager or Police Chief with this question. In brief, identify the points and places of pain and brokenness. This also involves discerning unresolved issues in such stronghold areas as iniquity, injustice, and immorality. While researchers

can gather this information, it is the servant leaders who are responsible to discern and decide what to do with it. I commend the work on the "exploration" phase of a movement as outlined by Glenn Barth in *The Good City*. (see Appendix, *"Reading Your City"*, Dr. Glenn Smith).

6. **Plan appropriate "catalytic kingdom events" for the Citywide Body.** Leaders are responsible to discern ways to deepen and broaden the movement in the hearts and minds of the "people in the pews." Such events may include citywide prayer and worship gatherings (see Appendix, "A Model Format for a Citywide Worship Gathering"), pulpit exchanges, cleaning up and repairing a local school, a food drive, outreach training seminars, etc. *Events can serve the helpful purpose of catalyzing increased organic unity from the outside-in.* Numerous movements have emerged out of a citywide outreach. Cooperation in such events creates a convergence of both organic and organizational unity that morphs into a more sustainable transformational vision.

7. **Engage in a collaborative partnership that serves a particular need in your city.** Often, several congregations will partner together on service projects, such as rejuvenating a school building, or putting on a "Convoy of Hope," or working with a Mayor's office on pressing issues of homelessness, affordable housing, Church-School partnerships,

and sex trafficking. The collaboration and positive outcomes of such endeavors builds trust and increased vision for further partnering. I was on-site in Tuscaloosa, Alabama for the birthing of The Hope Initiative, an inspired partnership between the Mayor and the leaders of the Tuscaloosa Prayer Network to target and transform the seven most broken down neighborhoods in the city. When the Lord of shalom and hope is in the equation, anything can happen.

Spiritual Leadership Roles

Ephesians 4 lists the five callings of leadership given to grow the church up into the fullness of the life of Christ: apostles, prophets, evangelists, pastors, and teachers. You may have noticed in my Royal Priesthood graphic, under "Core Components," I list "five-fold leadership." We have understood well the job descriptions of the pastor, teacher and evangelist. What has been far less understood are the roles of apostle and prophet. Twenty years into the city movement paradigm, there is admittedly a measure of controversy over these roles. I'm well aware of the "cessationist" perspective that holds that the roles of prophet and apostle have ceased since Jesus' incarnation and completion of the canon of Scripture. Personally, I don't believe Jesus "gave" the five offices after his ascension to build up the Church only to then "take back" the first two of them. But that said, the Old Testament prophets were unique, and served their purpose before Jesus came and the Bible was written. Likewise, the "apostles" who knew and walked with Jesus personally comprise a unique, one-of-a-kind category (including Paul, by virtue of personal revelation). It is not my aim in this book to provide a thorough discussion on this. But as it relates to birthing and building citywide transformational movements, let me share a few thoughts about the spiritual and functional roles of those who are given a prophetic or apostolic calling.

In many evangelical circles, just talking about the roles of apostle and prophet makes people nervous. Conversely, Charismatics and Pentecostals get frustrated having to walk on eggshells and apologize for what they consider God's provision of leadership for the Body of Christ. It has become clear to me that the birth and development of functional unity in the Body requires both a prophetic word (always consistent with the written word), and a leader of proven character, competence and authority. Whether we describe this role as "apostolic" or "catalytic," the function is the same: an appointing and anointing from the Lord to pioneer an expansion of the kingdom, and put in place a wineskin of kingdom community that is both organic and organizational.

I'm confident, in spite of the theological suspicions and tensions concerning these offices, that they are operative to put the Church in right order, restore it to health, and maximize the gifts and callings of the Holy Spirit. More and more, I am finding that among evangelical and conservative streams, while the "a-word" is not employed, the apostolic authority and function of mature leaders of influence is acknowledged. I don't want to oversimplify this, but as a practitioner, let me apply an analogy from the world of electricity. Whether we employ the word "catalytic" or "apostolic," leaders that ignite and sustain fruit-bearing movements need to operate on "A/C current," supernatural calling and empowerment. This is what Paul and Barnabas carried away from the Acts 13:1 moment in Antioch: an impartation to bring definition and health to the church in specific cities. Here's the reality: on the ground, in our cities, we have charismatics and evangelicals partnering for the greater glory of the Lord. Let's agree to disagree on the language and theology by which we describe such "point leaders," but find agreement on the function of God-appointed leadership.

In the context of the city movement, this "A/C current" leadership is typically provided in one of three ways: 1) in addition to leading a congregation, **a local pastor carries a mantle for citywide leadership 2) a small group of leaders submit to one another** in the form of a fellowship or council, typically loose and "ad hoc," with one among them taking the functional role of setting meetings and casting vision, and **3) someone comes in from the outside** to give occasional input, to consult, teach, and troubleshoot obstacles. Much of what I do in my visits is to encourage and mentor local leaders. The Spirit often gives me insight to see things and authority to say things that help bring definition, order, and fresh momentum. Here's my best, bottom line understanding. The Lord will select someone to receive *revelation of his will, give it clear articulation, then provide guidance for its effective activation in that particular context, most typically through a team in some form.*

Moving Forward

Here's a common challenge that can inhibit growing a movement forward. Most leaders are reticent to assert themselves over their peers, thinking, "Who am I to take city leadership?" Such a step may come off as self-promotion, pride, or posturing. Sometimes this deferential "walking on eggshells" goes on for years, short circuiting momentum. Sometimes a leader knows his call internally, having already heard from the Lord. Other times, peers may be the source of affirmation and encouragement. Sometimes there's a solo leader who hears the Holy Spirit and blows the trumpet. What I find most typical is a small core of two or three pastors, or a mix of pastors, non-profit or business leaders, who carry the seeds of this, who pray and say together, "What if others caught this vision and joined us? What could happen here?" This is a form of emergent leadership that is often interim in nature. Such a core typically becomes its own ad hoc envisioning team, refusing to let the vision fall to the ground. Any city that wants to move from a beachhead of hope toward spiritual breakthrough must have persevering leaders like this.

There's a critical point in this journey. A city may fail to formally acknowledge this new level of leadership, and fall back--back to events that have worked in the past, a monthly ministerial breakfast or lunch, prayer meetings that lack focus and fire, a Prayer Summit or leaders' retreat with diminished participation. Momentum lost is hard to re-gain.

Up to the present (mid 2013), I have held a conviction that some form of citywide leadership needs to be put in place. To be honest, however, this movement is still skewed towards a Western, "anglo" propensity to over-organize. But as of this writing, there are significant mega-shifts already underway: **1)** the transfer of leadership from the "boomer" generation to a mix of Gen-Ex and Millenial leaders, **2)** an increase of ownership and participation among ethnic leaders, and **3)** an increase of majority world global cities bringing contextual models into the mix. For now, suffice it to say we're in a new learning curve, addressing this question: "How does a more relational, organic group of leaders organize for maximum kingdom impact?" Millenials aren't keen on our structures, meetings and systems. Majority world leaders are understandably skeptical of Western structures. So, the jury is out on what ownership and leadership is going to look like going forward. Given the dizzying pace of cultural change, these new wineskins will be well in place, and dispensing a fresh vintage of kingdom wine before this book gets into print! This is a normal, healthy part of generational and cultural change.

Here's the bottom line. I believe there needs to be some form of leadership that stewards a gospel movement in a community, those who "wake up every day thinking about the city." Ideally, in the grid I have been grounded in, this should happen in a culture characterized by established relationships of trust and corporate prayer. At some point, a quorum that represents a cross section of city leaders must be present to "choose...men... who are known to be full of the Spirit and wisdom" (Acts 6:3). To be honest, pastors, non-profit and marketplace leaders are endowed with a distinctively different "dna." In most cities, leadership is weighted in one of these categories, most typically towards pastors. It is wise to be intentional broadening and balancing this mix, allowing the Royal Priesthood to be representative of the breadth of the local Body of Christ.

I certainly don't claim to have any "corner on the market of ideas" of what citywide leadership is to look like in your city. Honestly, in some places, leaders are skittish about more structure, and prefer to function more informally. In other settings, a trusted person or organization may step up and serve as a neutral, catalytic convener. I think all readers would readily agree that some form of biblical leadership is required to advance the kingdom. That's a given. But the form of such leadership must be flexible, and function effectively in each context. Visionary leaders will discern where and how the Spirit is moving, recruit and re-balance as needed, and implement changes. Now, let's move on to practical considerations involved in putting leadership of a citywide movement in place.

Chapter Five

Putting Citywide Leadership in Place

Mission Houston is one of the longest-running, best-led movements in the United States. In December 2009, Jim Herrington, one of the founders of this movement, asked and answered a question that gets to the core of city-reaching endeavors: "What will it really take to see your city transformed? God favoring and empowering the radical obedience of leaders that dare to follow God's design and ways for building his house." Jim also emphasized that this is an "inside-out" process. Leaders must be willing to be transformed agents before they can hope to serve as agents of external transformation. So, as we transition to talk about leadership structures, let's keep in mind that inward spiritual character is, and always should be, our highest priority and aim.

I'd like now to get specific on some of the pathways for transitioning from more traditional leadership structures to this new wineskin model of kingdom covenantal community. By observing the best practices of numerous movements over twenty-five years, we have gained some collective wisdom as to how functional leadership teams are put in place.

Common Scenarios for Putting Leadership into Place

1. **An existing ministerial association** of clergy gets a fresh vision of the citywide Body of Christ, and embraces a change of leadership to steward the revelation and continued growth of the "city church." Breaking this new ground does not typically make for an easy transition.

2. **A core of visionary leaders** emerges and begins to serve as an ad hoc group, promoting increased prayer, collaboration on missional endeavors, or evangelistic outreach. Often what I call an "Interim Envisioning Team" can function in this informal capacity for some time. But transitioning to a more formal team with widespread credibility can get "tricky." An outside, experienced facilitator can help make this transition.

3. **Often, we begin with a "coalition of the willing,"** a more informal group that serves to catalyze a new direction. These people typically increase the call to prayer and worship, sponsor teaching conferences, promote participation in a National Day of Prayer, convene a Leaders Prayer Summit or Kingdom Forum, or forge a partnership around a particular crisis or need in the city.

4. **Appointing of leaders of the city church by someone from the outside** who is walking in a mantle of catalytic leadership. Such a person is

assumed to have wide experience with emerging city movements, and has gained relational trust with a core of leaders in the city. This person moves in God's wisdom and discretion to put in place a city eldership represented by a diversity of congregations and organizations (often such an outside person assists in guiding a local group to self-select an initial team from among themselves).

5. **A major citywide event** (e.g., a Harvest Festival, evangelistic outreach, a worship event, a Willow Creek Leadership Summit, "Love and Respect" marriage workshop, etc.) has a success, and then continues on in some fashion on organizational "tracks." In this model, people have experienced the joy and synergy of walking and working together and want this cooperation to continue.

6 **A precipitating crisis, calamity or compelling social need** calls the citywide Body to mobilize a collaborative response. This necessitates an immediate trust and engagement in collaboration. Black and white leaders in the Tuscaloosa Prayer Network mobilized quickly to feed and house refugees from the ravages of Hurricane Katrina, and again with devastating tornados in the spring of 2011. Serve the City in Cedar Rapids found themselves quick responders to massive floods in the Spring of 2008. As we expect increased natural and social crises to hit our cities, there is no lead-time to prepare. In my view, the time and

opportunity is now to build relational infrastructure in Christ's Body, and lay down some preliminary plans for disaster relief. Folks in the Christian Emergency Network are available to help with this.

7. **Either a mega-church or non-profit organization** sponsors a Body-wide event, and becomes the de facto, functional leadership group in the city. In some cases, this leadership team then convenes a Leadership Prayer Summit, or calls in a spokesman from the city transformation paradigm to speak into the city. This scenario has its challenges. An existing leadership group will tend to a) have leaders that have become comfortable in their positions, b) exhibit tendencies toward top-down organization, and c) focus more on structured strategies and goals. In contrast, the "new wine" emerging in this paradigm calls for relationships that are organic and authentic, vision that is inspired by the Holy Spirit and a leadership style that is from the ground up.

8. **There is a "neutral convener,"** either a person or organization of significant influence that brings cohesion among the variety of kingdom assets in the city. Just up the road, in Portland, Oregon, the region-wide movement is functioning quite well without a defined leadership structure. The Luis Palau Association, based in Beaverton, has been successful implementing a model of "Seasons

of Service" to local communities, followed by a "Festival," with proclamation of the gospel. The LPA is now promoting contextual Church-School Partnerships, local congregations getting involved hands-on meeting both physical plant and educational needs in particular schools (information available at www.gospelmovements.com).

Regardless of how a citywide leadership emerges, it is wise to observe principles, patterns and best practices, and guard against looking for formulas. Each city has its own unique "dna," journey and pace of development. We must allow for variety and diversity in how the Spirit moves to establish servant leaders called to steward the citywide church. The structure of a leadership team is secondary. What is primary is a commitment to co-labor in the spirit of Jesus' teaching in John 15, allowing the Holy Spirit to stir and activate gifts and callings as he chooses.

Again, this is not an individual church, but a John 17 association of kindred hearts modeling a healthy "extended family." If Jesus' followers can walk in the Philippians 2 attitude of self-sacrifice, empowered by the Spirit, most *any* structure can work. Gary Schmitz, Director of Citywide Prayer in Kansas City puts it this way: "We proceed at the speed of trust."

The "Royal Priesthood:" A Leadership Matrix for City or Regional Transformational Movements

What might a "new wineskin of kingdom community" look like, and how does it function? As this is a wineskin still very much in process, any attempt to capture this will be incomplete and imperfect. But we've got to begin somewhere. The model below has been successfully implemented, and is functional in Kingston, Canada. In May, 2013 the leaders of greater Kansas City launched a Coalition based on this matrix. So, this is not just theory or a nice concept. I'm confident something similar to the structure I am envisioning is a step in the right direction, allowing for the freedom in each city or region to "tinker and tweak" with the model.

First, notice the first point under Core Components, "built on biblical, historic orthodoxy." In the early years, I often facilitated a process helping city teams identify common values, clarify vision and mission, etc. Invariably, the question of doctrine came up. It was typical for a team to assign a task group to come up with a doctrinal statement, then take a lot of time and energy haggling over agreement on points of historical, orthodox Christianity. My recommendation? Don't re-invent the doctrinal "wheel," but simply adopt a statement from another organization that broadly represents evangelical Christianity, e.g., NAE (National Association of Evangelicals), the Billy Graham Association, or the Lausanne Covenant. Other cities have gone with the Apostle's Creed. All of these will "nail down" the primary points of doctrinal truth essential to define your movement as biblically "orthodox." I adhere to St. Augustine's wisdom from early Church history:

Putting Citywide Leadership in Place

"In things essential, unity. In things non-essential, tolerance. In all things, love." John Wesley quoted this maxim often. If we allow such things as eschatology, sacraments, or gifts of the Holy Spirit to divide us, an authentic John 17 witness of oneness will remain a distant dream.

Let me say again, though there are principles and patterns, each movement, given its unique assets, has freedom to envision and contextualize what their leadership structure will look like. There is no "cookie cutter" approach for functional leadership in a city seeking to embrace this new wineskin. Having introduced this matrix in my Prologue, I encourage you to take a few moments now to reflect on it more carefully.

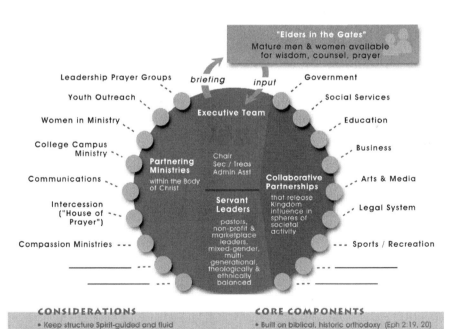

For larger graphic, see the appendix page 279

What I'm envisioning here is a roundtable, a grassroots, egalitarian group of servant leaders committed to partnering a sustained release of kingdom influence and impact in all spheres of societal activity. *The intentional aim must be towards a team that is mixed-gender, multi-generational, theologically diverse and ethnically balanced.* Realistically, this is not always achievable in the short-term. This is an asset-based model. It cannot be rushed. Rather, we must ask and allow the Holy Spirit to raise up participants in his way and time. Wise, "early adopter" leadership will pray and watch for emerging team prospects, and add them according to the principle, "it seemed right to the Holy Spirit and to us." This kind of leadership wineskin must be organic and fluid, allowing for busy, competent assets to step in, or off, as determined by their circumstances, and the leading of the Spirit.

Leaders called to a team like this serve in four spheres, **1) "elders in the gates"** (mature, trusted advisors), **2) the executive team** (functional leaders at the core), **3) partnering ministries within the Body of Christ** (examples of this noted on the graphic), and **4) leaders of collaborative partnerships** that release kingdom influence into the community. Each leader sitting at this table is challenged to recruit his or her own cadre of leaders to implement transformational ministries in their specific area. That leader is then responsible in regular meetings (I recommend monthly), through both written and verbal reporting, to keep the wider roundtable appraised of progress, new initiatives, challenges, resource needs, etc. These leaders function according to "delineation of passion," i.e., their heart beats for that particular area, and serves as a magnet to attract others. Track with me as I explain the role and function of each of these groups.

Elders in the Gates

"Elders in the Gates" play a vital role shaping this model. These individuals may be fully active or semi-retired pastors, elders, leaders of non-profits or prayer leaders, respected men and women of wisdom committed to the vision of city transformation. While they may not have the time or energy to functionally sit at the table, their wisdom, input and intercessory covering are essential. Often, when conversations arise about covering from "fathers of the city," it is a nice idea, but goes nowhere. Someone needs to take the time to connect with the patriarchs and matriarchs of your movement, draw them in and invite their inputs. They are a virtual reservoir of godly wisdom. It is assumed the "Executive Team" has either regular or occasional connection with these individuals, and seeks often their counsel and intercession.

The Executive Core Team

Functionally, an Executive Team is necessary for efficiently moving forward. Typically, this is comprised of five to seven persons, and includes a point person (facilitator) who serves a year term, which may be renewable. In some cases, if the point leader is effective, and has time and energy for the role, he or she may remain at point indefinitely. But it is also possible to rotate this function. This must be someone with proven character and a skill-set conducive to leading other strong leaders of influence. Secondly, I prefer to see a paid, part-time administrative assistant fulfill the duties of taking minutes, keeping the database current, receipting financial donations, and putting out timely and creative communications. I recommend a well designed website or blog, a creative e-bulletin format and use of social media. And third, it is helpful to have Executive Team members who oversee the two major areas--partnering ministries within the Body, and collaborative partnerships that reach into the community. Personally, in my consultation, I steer away from old paradigm designations of President, Vice President, Secretary, etc. I believe we can keep this biblical, simple and flexible, letting the Holy Spirit guide as he wills.

Here's another common question: "To incorporate, or not to incorporate?" Of course an existing 501-C-3 non-profit church or organization can function as the legal and fiduciary entity, allowing an emerging movement to get up and running. But if the movement has life, and participation grows, it is advisable to apply for its own non-profit status.

Partnering Ministries Within the Body of Christ

In the Old Testament context, this would be the "Ezra" component, priestly/pastoral ministries at all levels of kingdom life. Any given community will have its distinctive assets that operate within the local church sphere. To most of us, this is where we are most familiar. Since Corvallis has been my local "laboratory" for over thirty years, here's a sampling of partnering ministries that are citywide. We have had a successful Love, INC, a citywide compassion clearing house, up and running for twelve years (the majority of evangelical churches and non-profits support Love, INC). One of our stronger congregations puts on an annual Fall Jubilee teaching conference for the women of our region. Our Youth Pastors often do things collaboratively. In Spring

2013 they put on "Redeem My City," training middle and High School students to redeem their scholastics, athletics, sexuality, social media, with a greater vision to impact their city. One brother on our team has been the catalyst for unity and collaboration among the campus ministries at Oregon State University. Recently, there is healthy partnering to reach an increased number of international students., a virtual diaspora that has come to our doorstep. We have a strong, local "House of Prayer," men and women who regularly invite God's presence and favor into our community. Over the course of two decades, kingdom leaders in our city have developed a culture of partnering. *Here's the simple pattern: simply watch for what the Spirit of God is touching, and look for champions who own, organize and lead to meet a need.* Here's my word of wisdom. Don't try to create or "push" partnering ministries. Just discern what God is doing in your city, look for the champion(s), and engage the journey of kingdom synergy!

Collaborative Partnerships

Again, in the context of Old Testament revelation, this is the "Nehemiah" component, vocational practitioners engaged in commerce, government, education, arts, media, etc. Increasingly we need to look outside the congregational structures of church and release champions who have influence to bring transformational change to the "marketplace." This could mean partnering with a Mayor on low-cost housing for the poor, or providing life skills and vocational training for the disadvantaged, or mentoring at-risk children in our schools. As a team of leaders stewarding a wider vision for our city, we cannot just keep building better relationships with one another and laboring in prayer while the walls and gates of our city are broken. Yes, *we build an on-going, healthy culture of kingdom koinonia, but we also roll up our sleeves and engage full on in "anointed activism."* Remember, both Jesus and Peter shared the same observation about the power of good deeds: "let your light shine before men, that they may see your good deeds and praise your Father in heaven" (Mt. 5:16; cf. 1 Pe. 2:12). *So, as practitioners, I believe we take a "both, and" approach. We build the Body of Jesus Christ up in love, we let our light shine in the dark places in our cities with good deeds, and we commit to a daily, sustainable lifestyle of loving not-yet-believers towards the kingdom.*

You are looking here for life and champions *outside* the church walls: business leaders, a police chief, Ph.D. professor on campus, a physician, or attorney. This is where this wineskin is exploding with life and vision, where members of the Royal Priesthood are waking up and showing up for duty, ready to release the life-giving power of the gospel into the spheres of local government, educational institutions, the courts, the local Chamber of Commerce. Since I began leading Summits and kingdom Forums in Abilene, Texas in 2010, Stan, the Chief of Police, has been enthusiastically present at every meeting! At the last gathering, he brought the Fire Chief and a city councilor. Again, don't fall prey to a pressure to "create" these collaborations. As a leadership team, seek the Lord regularly, asking him to raise up men and women with voice and influence within their vocational spheres. It is better to grow and develop two to three such partnerships than to over-reach and fall short of expectations.

As a biblical theologian, my "re-set button" always returns to Solomon's proven wisdom: "Unless the Lord builds the house, its builders labor in vain" (Ps. 127:1).

For a city team member, here are the *basic, bottom-line expectations:* **1) make the monthly meeting a high priority, 2) be consistent participating in regular prayer times with kingdom colleagues, 3) engage with citywide initiatives, and 4) invest time fulfilling specific task group responsibilities,** or delegate them to others. In my opinion, I think the character qualities required for a church elder outlined in 1 Timothy 3 and Titus 2 should be required of members of a city leadership team. But the specific requirements, "husband of one wife…able to teach," should not be required. These are requirements specific to a local church congregation. This level of leadership is neither a congregation nor denomination. As a body, it can exercise no binding spiritual authority over anyone in the city. It cannot formally discipline anyone who errs. This group stewards a wider work of unity, prayer and collaboration, and leads by influence, not by governmental authority. The group could aptly be described as an "association" of like-minded colleagues laboring across a city or region for a common purpose. Thus, women, marketplace leaders, and unmarried lay ministers may be involved.

I recommend intentional, frequent interface among team members to keep building deeper relationships, to worship together, and to dialogue about the unfolding vision for the city. As challenging as this is, it's important to keep these teams on the same "vision page," and at a similar pace. Thus, I highly recommend an annual team retreat, ideally, an overnight, comprising at least twenty-four hours. But a full day retreat, at a local venue, can also be effective. While it is okay to prepare an agenda and talking points, the highest priorities are to deepen relationships, and inquire of the Lord: *"Where are you moving in our city? Where are you bringing people together to touch a targeted need?"* Take time to listen to the Holy Spirit, and one another. Take time to discern and assess the weak places on the wall of your community. Times like this can have productive results, with a diverse team of leaders coming to that sweet spot, "It seemed right to the Holy Spirit and to us."

As we continue to develop innovative models, it is the quality and commitment of leaders that determines whether a citywide movement sustains momentum, or stagnates. I believe the Lord is watching and waiting to do his part--to release the presence and power of his Spirit--if we will rise up and be obedient to do our part. We can only do our best to offer ourselves to Jesus, and allow him, the Chief Architect, to place the diversity of living stones when and where he wills.

This leadership matrix is a template in process. Take of it what you find clarifying and helpful, and tweak what is not. In the art of contextualizing truth that is eternal, it is vital to not fixate on structure, but to fix our eyes on kingdom principles, and courageously obey the leading of the Holy Spirit.

Facing Hard Issues

As we move in these new directions, there may be issues that arise, and adjustments that need to be made. It all can look great on paper, but we're dealing with the unpredictability of human personalities who are interpreting and processing a new paradigm. I want to touch on six key issues that commonly emerge.

1. **Moving the from local to city church.** This is another major hurdle. This is why I devoted Chapter 3 to this topic. I will bring a succinct summary here. In some environments, change of thinking can come to a large number of leaders within a matter of months. In other cities, it may take years for local pastors to see and value the vision. Getting a vision for the inherent oneness of the Body of Christ in a city takes revelation. We cannot expect to persuade and convince anyone, whether pastor or organizational leader, to broaden his horizon of ministry beyond his own backyard. We also have to account for different personality types. Some leaders have a minimal felt need for intimate relationships. Others may receive relational benefit from their denominational stream. And most are always overloaded with the needs of their own congregation. For many varied reasons, local colleagues choose to self-select out of the mix. So, it is important that we bless them and their ministries, and ask God to continue to illumine them with a revelation of a healthy, Ephesians 4 Body functioning across the city.

Let me say this again. *The citywide church does not supplant the local church in any way,* but rather expresses the biblical reality that there is one Body that finds expression in a diversity of congregations. In any city, the central question needs to be, "How can we work together to more effectively reach our city with the gospel?" These clear biblical mandates alone provide a compelling case for busy pastors to justify the expense of time and energy outside of their local congregations.

It is also helpful to provide books and videos that unfold what God is doing in cities today. The Luis Palau Evangelistic Association has significantly caught the vision that the greatest potential for outreach and kingdom advance is happening in the context of the city movement, and launched www.gospelmovements.com, providing stories, resources and tools to city practitioners. Similarly, leaders of transformational movements throughout Australia launched www.oneheart.com.au. Tim Keller, in his twenty-seven minute closing plenary at the 2012 Movement Day succinctly and stunningly nails the distinctives that should characterize the "city church" (www.movementday.com). It may often take another voice that resonates with a busy leader and validates wider involvement in a city church expression.

2. **Affirming and holding servant leaders accountable.** Other leaders may struggle submitting to the authority of such a servant leader "council." Church denominational structures might also be suspicious. Non-participating pastors or churches might say, "Who are *you* to discern vision for *my* church and

priorities for *our* ministries?" This is a fair question. Whether anyone verbalizes such concerns, you can be sure they will have them.

However, this kind of citywide leadership is not a new kind of governmental authority, but rather an association of kingdom men and women who wisely spend their influence capital in recruiting others to more effectively reach their community with the gospel. Servant leaders are aware that they are part of a move of the Holy Spirit to restore unity and vitality to the Body of Christ in accord with Jesus' priestly prayer. And because they see themselves as directly accountable to Jesus, which includes all the churches, they also see themselves as accountable to their peers in those churches as they present vision or strategies. Their focus is on healthy "body parts," individual congregations growing in the Spirit, and corporately submitting to the Head when there is a call to mobilize in a service project or display a witness of oneness.

3. **Achieving racial, cultural, and theological diversity.** This also is an ongoing challenge that requires constant vigilance and forbearance. Honestly, this is difficult. It is easy enough to believe and say that "we are one in Christ." But when we try to walk in functional unity, the stress lines show up. In urban, multi-ethnic settings, it is advisable to begin building authentic relationships in the early stages. Leaders of different class and color must mutually own and steward a vision for the city church. This all sounds well and good, but many key leaders may not be

convinced that this "new thing" is really of God. You can do the best you can to honor the diversity of the Body, and draw leaders in that represent all the various streams. But--and let's please get this--it is unwise to cave in to an obligatory "tokenism." Any arm-twisting to enlist token support will be superficial and short-lived. Building authentic city leadership that is truly diverse is a labor that takes blood (the blood of Jesus!), sweat, tears...and years! But, to honor our Head, and to qualify as a concrete answer to his priestly prayer in John 17:21-23, it is worth the work!

I was privileged to walk with a mix of black and white leaders in Tuscaloosa, Alabama for ten years. This is where Gov. George Wallace stood on the campus of the University of Alabama in the early 1960's, proclaiming arrogantly, "There will be no black students on this campus!" I have to say, the early prayer gatherings from 1993-95 were "raw" as these leaders got real dealing with racism that was both personal, and systemic to Southern culture. But out of this crucible where honesty and unpacking pain became normative, the Tuscaloosa Prayer Network was birthed. Truthfully, though far from perfect and still in process, these brothers and sisters walk in the sweetest, most genuine mixed racial fellowship I have seen in the American context.

We just need to do our best to be inclusive from the beginning, but without compromising the core requirements of the role of a servant leader. Ultimately, we all really *do* need one another! At a recent meeting of city-reaching leaders, one participant shared this encouraging insight: "*As we walk more together, we will wear off one another's eccentricities, and fill up one another's deficiencies.*"

4. **The question of women in governmental leadership.** Can women be considered to serve on a citywide leadership team? Even if it is determined theologically that they *can,* is it advisable in every context? The debate on the role of women in governmental leadership continues unabated, with both theological and cultural implications.

Many excellent books, with sound exegesis, open the door for women to serve as pastors and leaders. On the other hand, the Southern Baptist Convention closed the theological door on women pastors in 2000. Some denominations (mainline, evangelical, charismatic, Pentecostal) freely ordain women pastors. In African-American and Hispanic cultures, I often meet husband and wife co-pastors, or women moving freely as pastor-teachers. Because of the diversity of hermeneutic interpretation of biblical texts as well as cultural differences, we're just going to have to continue to live with this tension, irrigate it with a lot of love and prayer, and patiently work it out in each context.

Well-meaning, sincere Christians are on both sides of this fence, with most of us leaning one way or the other, not altogether certain what the Bible really *does* say on this matter. I know of many cities where the mere idea of a woman in governmental leadership stirs division. In these places, it's just not wise to press the issue. My bottom line:

let the context and the consensus of corporate theological wisdom. Seek God's mind, decide, and walk it out in love.

In settings where women are allowed and affirmed to serve, some male leaders still may have theological reservations, or still may be very much in process with their position, but because of their commitment to a citywide movement, they welcome the participation of women in leadership. Most of us have "litmus tests," measures of orthodoxy, personal preferences and opinions. But in choosing to honor one another and walk together in the wider Body, we can go two ways: we can be forbearing on an issue of secondary doctrinal importance, or defer to those who are unable to accept women in governmental leadership, and avoid division over the issue. Clearly, the Spirit is superintending and blessing both options as movements continue to develop. Ultimately, only the Lord himself can arbitrate the interpretive obscurities and complexities of this issue resident in his word. Personally, when the Spirit guided me to put a citywide leadership in place in my own city in 1999, I insisted that we include at least one woman. We ended up with two. One was the acknowledged "pastor" to women leaders in the city, the other was Director of our citywide compassion ministry supported by 90% of our evangelical congregations. There have been no ripples or ramifications of this inclusion now for fourteen years.

5. **Different approaches to evangelism and discipleship.** Being alongside various leaders in a lot of cities, I have found it is easy to assume everyone around the table would get excited about the idea of increased

collaboration on outreach and discipleship. I used to say something like this, "We're not competing for the same market share here. We have a shared responsibility to win and disciple the unbelieving souls in our city." Well, that sounds great, but it does not work all that well in the trenches. Pastors and elders--Southern Baptists, independent charismatic, Presbyterian, Evangelical Free, you-name-it—have their own philosophy and approach to winning souls and assimilating them into their congregation. They may also have an aggressive strategy for planting other churches that fit their denominational distinctives. This is just the way it is. Sure, a diversity of churches and outreach or service organizations may come together for a city or regional outreach, but inevitably *each congregation has its own distinctive vision and passion to reach people with the gospel, and grow their church into a healthy Body.* So, to step up on my soapbox again, and offer my three-legged stool: in healthy city movements, we call leaders to 1) build authentic, covenant relationship with one another (Jo. 17:21-23), 2) engage in transformational prayer that is regular and corporate (1 Ti. 2:1-3), and 3) partner—by choice, not by coercion—on collaborative kingdom endeavors focused on sharing the good news and doing good works.

The reality is, a good shepherd and faithful elders in any given congregation will want to grow *their* church, and will have their own innovative approaches to doing just that. We simply need to bless that initiative and diversity, and allow for each congregation or ministry non-profit to buy into whatever citywide initiatives they choose to track with.

6. **Personnel and funding.** In the early stages, there often is a lot of excitement and energy flowing into the new endeavor. After the initial dust settles, however, there comes a reality check when servant leaders reach the limitations of their own time and energy. It is easy to say, "Funding will always flow towards a valid vision." But casting and implementing a compelling vision takes work, boots on the ground. Men and women called to the pastorate are consumed day and night with the primary care of their flocks. Leaders of non-profits also have limits on their time, often mandated by their supervisory staff. Marketplace leaders often get pulled back into priority demands of their vocation. And all busy leaders are always having to build in time and energy to sustain healthy marriages and families.

In my opinion, an administrative assistant/communications director operating at ten to fifteen hours a week is a minimum for getting a movement up and running. Increasing numbers of cities are now looking for funding earlier in the process, and are typically raising money for a full-time city movement coordinator, and a part-time administrative assistant. Realistically, the innovators and early adopters should be challenged earlier on to sow financially into the emerging wineskin. Most teams begin by funding the person who has the passion, time and energy to develop a Body-wide ministry and enlist greater ownership/participation. Any movement serious about growing to the next level would be wise to employ, paid or volunteer, someone with proven expertise on setting up a business and funding plan. In reality, funding a full time city movement coordinator is a hard sell. In most situations I see, the passion for John 17 oneness of the Body of Christ compels volunteer participation.

Discerning Contextual Strategies

Whatever structural form your city leadership takes, if it is indeed serving as a true "Royal Priesthood," those so engaged will be regularly seeking the Lord for strategies to more effectively reach the people of their city. There will be a widespread mix of perspectives on both the nature and means of "transformation." For example, the movement in New York City is highly intentional and strategic with a church planting strategy. Jim Herrington is engaged in Houston with making disciples in the marketplace who are self-reproducing. Leaders in Phoenix have chosen to eliminate child hunger and place children in foster care. In view of the diversity of on-the-ground approaches, I provide a "bird's eye view" of seven general approaches in the Appendix (A Sampling of Transformational Strategies).

Any city, particularly those over 100,000 in population, will have numerous "players and layers of kingdom activity." Through the increase of social media, we may assume there will be multiple connections in any given city to a variety of proponents of transformational change. *Trying to call the Body of Christ to a singular strategy to share good news and do good works is a noble idea, but making it work on the ground is daunting.* Sure, it's a wonderful thing for a citywide leadership team to get consensus on God's mind, land on a strategy, and recruit participation.

But here's another observation, forged in the crucible of reality. Each city has its own organic identity, a sense of "we," a geographic and cultural uniqueness. While a city's spiritual gatekeepers may be inspired by another city's story or an event or strategy that worked somewhere else, they want to engage in something distinctive in *their* own city. This mindset is neither wrong nor self-centered. It is not even competitive. It's just the way it is. *With all the data available on what's already happening, and how to advance a process of transformation, the leadership of the movement, however it is structured, will ultimately select the kind of approach that seems to fit their city best, implement it, and call it their own.* As this wineskin continues to grow, the "cross fertilization" of ideas and practices is healthy.

This movement is a "work in progress." I believe we are steadily moving toward a holistic paradigm of transformational change, informed increasingly by Scripture, empowered by the Holy Spirit, and applied by faithful men and women in their own local laboratories. *In short, what I see developing are contextual, custom-made applications that are syncretistic (a combination of various components) and synergistic (a variety of approaches and "players" that complement one another).*

While this may sound chaotic and seem competitive, this is often the reality on the ground. I find this both challenging, and exhilarating. Why? Because "God is at work" in our cities, reaching out to the lost and showing mercy to the least. And he works in a multitude of ways, through a diversity of "royal priesthood" assets. *We dare not presume to categorize the what and the how of divine prerogatives! Find the life-giving presence of God in your city, join it, and call others to it.* Let's just welcome the wonder and marvel of our Lord's mercy, and have freedom to steer clear of our propensity to have a "program or plan." Let's understand that there is no "one size fits all" strategy for city movements. For sure there are valuable principles to discern, ways in which we observe God at work among his people. While the graces are the same, the places and applications will differ.

Here's an illustration. Platte City, MO is one of the "village fire" cities connected to the movement that is growing in the greater Kansas City area. Pastor and point man Michael Lazio has sown his entire adult life into his city, building that core covenantal kingdom community I've been describing through this book. Over many years, the Platte City pastors have prayed together, for one another, and for an increase of the kingdom in their region. Daily, in the local Bethel House of Prayer, saints have sought God's favor for their city. And Michael has cultivated a Philippians 2 culture of leaders honoring and preferring one another through exchanging pulpits, sharing meals and coffees, taking fishing trips together. What has been faithfully sown into this soil is now resulting in a season of reaping.

On December 8, 2012, Michael and his colleagues launched their first "Day of Hope," a smaller scale one-day event patterned after the Convoy of Hope. These folks took a strategic model, and modified it to fit their culture and context. This was a collaborative partnership between the social sector (churches and non-profits), private sector (businesses) and the public sector (schools, medical clinics, governmental agencies), all aimed at helping people with economic, medical and family needs. Congregations partnering with the Platte County Health Department, the school district, Heartland Health Clinic, Rotary and Lions Clubs, the Chamber of Commerce, the YMCA, Walgreens, Walmart, the Platte Valley Bank, etc. Here are just a few grace gifts offered on the inaugural "Day of Hope:" a Holiday Meal Box with a $20 gift card from Farmland Meats, Walmart gift cards, hygiene packs, medical and dental exams, family photographs, winter coats, hats, gloves and home made blankets, a Christmas store with toys for kids. Everyone received the Jesus DVD. God's local Royal Priesthood, sharing good deeds and opening hearts to the good news of the gospel.

Out of this has sprung a new non-profit, The Days of Hope Foundation, to continue an on-going ministry to needy families in Platte County. Day of Hope #2 is on the radar for December 7, 2013. This is a sustainable, contextual strategy, a united, praying, caring Body of Jesus reaching out in compassion, touching lives on the ragged fringe of society. So, let's turn a corner and explore how to better forge kingdom partnerships that honor the Lord, and bear fruit for his glory.

Chapter Six

Expanding Collaborative Kingdom Partnerships in Your City

I want to begin with two working assumptions. First, you may already be up and running with some form of citywide leadership team, and ready to forge some partnerships that more effectively release gospel impact into your city. Second, there are probably informal, Spirit-led partnerships already formed or forming at the grassroots, persons or organizations that have relational trust, and resonate on a common mission. I'll be addressing both models.

First, an illustration from the trenches. Back in the mid-1990's, I was facilitating a gathering of leaders in a major city on the East Coast. As we moved into a time of prayer, I slid to the outer circle and sat with a couple of business leaders who had been invited by their pastors. The conversation turned sour. "These guys" (pastors) don't have the skill-sets, competence and time to effectively lead the kind of city movement they're talking about here. Truth is, they're holding back the kind of leaders you need to get something done in this city." This comment underscores *a problem common to transformational movements: inability to get a variety of leaders, gifts and callings working together in synergy.*

Later that day, I processed these comments with the pastors who had invited me into the city. Here was their response: "These are really great guys, but they are just not spiritually mature enough to lead something like this. They don't spend much time praying and they always want to run off and do a project of some sort." That was fifteen years ago. We're in a new world. The current buzz is all about "cross sector collaboration," partnering across the boundaries between Public, Private and Social spheres. So, who makes and takes the time to get leaders with radically different "operating systems" on the same page? In this chapter I want to engage this topic: *"how does a variety of gifts, callings, ethnicities and personalities really function on the ground in any given city or regional context?"*

What's the Mission?

Whether a mega-city of millions, or a "burg" of thousands, this comes down to real people in real places doing the hard work building trust, engaging in regular prayer and offering themselves as conduits for God's presence that permeates all spheres of societal activity. This is about uniting, equipping and mobilizing Christ's Body to leverage its influence. Let me be clear. In this chapter I'm focusing on the "Nehemiah like" collaborative partnerships that get outside of the walls of the Church and reach into our culture. There are a variety of ways in which these partnerships form. I'm going to talk about two: 1) formal initiatives launched by a citywide leadership team, and 2) more informal, Spirit-led collaborations that form between individuals or ministries that have common capital of trust and mission. Both are welcome and complementary, especially if there is good communication and coordination among kingdom leaders on the ground.

In the last two chapters, we looked at what leadership of a city church might look like, and how to implement it. Here my focus is functional, *how does a city transformational movement mobilize a diversity of "living stones" to serve as a "royal priesthood," bringing kingdom presence to the doorsteps of daily life in a city?* Truthfully, each one of us is stuck inside his or her own "grid." We assemble alongside one another, seemingly connected, but operate with distinctly different mental maps. So, asking the question in theological language, how do we functionally bring together the unique callings and skill-sets of priests, prophets and kings? Even if parties reach a common understanding on mission, you face another challenge: getting them to work together to *implement.* I have come to believe that we must welcome a healthy cross-fertilization of dissimilar ideas and applications, like tossing post-it notes on a wall in a brainstorming session. So, when you get a mixed gender, multi-generational group of pastors, business leaders, intercessors, and serving ministries in a room talking about "who we are and what we're doing together," you step over the threshold from manageable to miracle.

Forging Collaborative Partnerships

Engaged in the city-reaching movement for the past thirty-three years, I have been a disciple/learner, an apprentice of the Holy Spirit, discerning month-to-month God's design for functional John 17 communities. I've had numerous opportunities for "on-the-job training." Through many painful presumptions and mistakes, the Spirit has sharpened my discernment and honed skills for getting people tracking together and forging partnerships. Then the book *Well Connected* dropped into my world, confirming what I had been learning through intuition. In my view, Phill Butler, Director of Vision Synergy, in Lynnwood Washington, is a "master teacher" in this area of collaborative partnerships. Here's my advice to any serious city transformational practitioner: read the book, and glean Phill's nuggets. No one needs labor to re-inventing this wheel!

Butler points out a huge and helpful distinction between partnering and networking. A plethora of congregations, outreach organizations, serving ministries are all about sharing the gospel and serving people's needs, with their own bent towards a particular demographic or neighborhood. Here is Butler's observation: "No single partnership can ever hope to reach/serve these widely varying special needs/interests. This suggests that any effort at a citywide initiative will probably be best structured as a network—not a partnership. Networks exist to help individual ministries with a common vision do their own individual work better."

Getting specific about partnerships, here's an illuminating quotation from one of the first iterations of Vision Synergy's 2007 training manual:

> "It is not about just getting it started and running on the excitement of this brave new world of partnership;

rather, it is the 'discipline of getting things done' in a highly diverse team of folk working on a very complex set of problems in a very dynamic and interdependent city environment from within stable and independent organizations. It is a ridiculous working situation that one might normally avoid. At the end of the day, however, *there really are things that need to be done that must be done together and it really does take a system to change a system.* Thus, the effort and training required to not only sustain a partnership but to see it thrive are truly eternal investments."

If our aim is to catalyze and sustain a life-transforming work of the Holy Spirit in our cities, we must understand the depth of complexity of the social, political and economic systems that permeate a city culture. Likewise, we must then understand that the Body of Christ (a spiritual society interspersed throughout a multiplicity of city systems) must get its "system" together by engaging the sacrifice and hard work involved in building partnerships that release the positive leaven of kingdom influence into the city. A superior system, empowered by God's Spirit, engaging and changing systems energized and perpetuated over generations by the fallibility and falleness of humankind.

Forging Productive Partnerships: Essential Components

What follows are seven action steps that I have learned to employ in cities where I've been invited in to coach. While I don't claim these steps to be comprehensive, they are inclusive of core elements needed to build kingdom partnerships that result in measureable outcomes. Again, these components can be applicable to both formal city team initiatives or to more informal, grassroots partnering. Having walked a lot of miles on this road in many cities, we dare not try to be overly prescriptive or controlling of the sovereign and of times surprising work of God's Spirit.

1. Provide an on-going context in which to build increased trust in relationships.

Beginning with leaders of influence, we need to break down walls of suspicion and competition, and build bridges of trust. This necessitates a context of some sort where busy leaders take time to listen to and hear one another. I offer three suggestions for a context like this that enhances relational cohesion. First, I know of no context better than spending extended time in God's presence with colleagues, worshiping, praying, bearing one another's burdens in small groups, taking time to listen to one another and giving the Spirit opportunity to stir fresh vision. I believe this involves the vertical component, inviting the Lord into the equation. But this is also a horizontal dynamic, with skilled facilitation that fosters open communication and understanding.

A second format I have employed successfully is the Kingdom Forum, a half day, typically a Saturday morning, where marketplace leaders, pastors, non-profits and government officials share their vision for how they see the kingdom increasing in the city. In one community, the point leader convened three Forums in a downtown hotel, allowing wide participation. A third approach is the Focus Group, in most cases an evening, where this same mix of believer-priests engage the vision of city transformation, sharing ideas and open dialogue, listening to one another and coming to consensus. Whatever vehicle you use, building increased trust and cohesion in relationships is a work of the Holy Spirit. Wise leaders will provide some form of context for unhurried, honest communication, well facilitated and saturated with prayer.

2. **Develop a common language that connects participants.**

I have learned firsthand the value of open forums and roundtables in which participants are invited to share ideas and inputs focusing on a particular theme. Ideally, this involves a mix of the "royal priesthood" (see Chap. 5), a diversity of those serving as kingdom salt and light in the city. I often begin a "Kingdom Forum" inviting participants to share "milestones of remembrance," markers of the Lord's faithfulness to his people and to their city. This is a simple celebration of God's goodness, putting on a whiteboard or powerpoint a spiritual history that provides a backdrop leading up to the present. Invariably, many in the room are unaware of much of this history, and are amazed to learn of successes and breakthroughs. With a number of markers on the board, we then go vertical, thanking heavenly Father for what he has already done.

I often then pose two questions: "What do you see God doing in your community?" Then, "What is the pain/injustice in your city where a united Body of Christ could help to bring healing?" Give sufficient time to this session, scribing responses on a whiteboard, leaving room for others to confirm or amplify any given observation. Here's another approach: ask two or three leaders, known for their unique service in particular spheres of the community, to take ten to fifteen minutes to share their calling and unpack their concerns. This can take the form of praise to God for good things on the radar, or "in your face" problems that cry for attention.

I might also ask: "Where do you feel God's heart breaking in your city? (the Nehemiah component, assessing the "rubble"). Some typical issues: affordable housing, helping with the homeless, providing life and financial skills training, assisting a local school system with their physical plants, or providing mentoring for at-risk children. In many cities, a small group of leaders representing the evangelical community book a meeting with the Mayor, and pose the question: "What are some of the needs of our city that are not being adequately met from government resources? What are you most personally concerned about? How can we help?" Over two decades, I have heard of very few Mayors who have refused prayer or turned help away when offered.

Towards the end of the Forum, I typically list the most pressing needs on the city's radar, and ask: "Where do we need to improve our service? How can we work better at partnering in this area, sharing personnel and resources?" Even if we find consensus on one or two initiatives, we're gaining ground! In one city where I led this process, within five minutes a task group was formed on the spot to work together on sex trafficking issues. As we look at potential initiatives, I may ask participants to "vote" for the top three needs they see on the board, and prioritize them from top down. This gives a group freedom to assess current reality, own responsibility for specific points of pain and commit to any specific assignments going forward. Here is a significant point of learning: where participants are given a hand to design something, they will have a heart to own and implement the solution.

In the settings of both the Leadership Encounters and Kingdom Forums, participants with a different "wiring" and gifting begin to develop a common language, a rubric that is helpful for understanding what we are wanting to do together. In my experience, this process is measured in years, not months. It may take multiple Encounters or frequent Forums and Focus Groups to get a diversity of players on the same paradigm page!

3. Achieve consensus on your vision and mission.

You may already have a seasoned citywide or regional leadership team up and running. Or, you may look more like what I described earlier as an "interim envisioning team." You may feel like a "rag-tag bunch of like-minded radicals," an informal group looking to better organize your leadership. You may be two pastoral colleagues with a burden to adopt a school down the street. You may be a pastor in dialogue with the Chief of Police talking about partnering on a chaplaincy program.

Whatever your situation or stage of development, whether formal or informal, you're already wrestling with the question, *"Who are we, and what's our mission?"* Defining *"mission"* must be concrete, getting to "what" we are about.

In one city where I coached, the group came up with this simple mission statement: "Worshiping the Lord, Uniting the Church, Serving our Community." Keep it simple and compelling. Whether we like it or not, we're in the era of the reduced sound and visual bite. Down the road in Eugene, OR, the One Hope Network landed on this: "Joining Together to Show Jesus' Love." Just recently, a movement in Phoenix took shape: Our Mission: One church Serving the Valley, Our Vision: No Child Uncared for in the Valley, Our Strategy: Adopt every School, Eradicate hunger, Empty Foster care. The emerging kingdom coalition has consensus on its first shared missional endeavor.

If you do a reasonably good job communicating the mission, you will quickly attract other innovators and early adopters. As you grow, it gets more challenging as you build a wider coalition of the willing. But you will find that both leaders and lay workers are attracted to "life." When people see an increasingly healthy Body of Christ working together, they will want to be a part of it. Living your passion, letting the Psalm 133 and John 17 "dna" shine through, will always be compelling. Sharing stories about God healing broken lives, people coming into the kingdom, putting a roof on a widow's home, or volunteers from numerous churches renovating a school building in a day, this is what we're really about.

4. Assign roles and responsibilities

When forging a partnership, my preference is to emphasize organic (life) over organization (structure), following the leading of the Holy Spirit, and making decisions through prayer, discussion and consensus. Operating in a framework of biblical leadership like this is currently working very well in numerous city movements. A wider challenge is getting more rank-and-file, everyday believers involved in these partnerships. One of my more practical colleagues is always saying, "down and out, let's get this down and out!" In other words, getting folks at the grassroots engaged hands-on. When you successfully mobilize church attenders to get "out of their seats and into the streets" serving together, you are seeing significant breakthrough.

Whether we are talking formal city team or more informal partnering, a clear definition of roles and responsibilities is important. I advise teams in the early stages to do an assessment of assets, either formal or informal. Here's the question: What passion, skill-set or competency do you bring to this team? Where do you see yourself investing your influence and time promoting partnerships that will advance kingdom influence in our city? An initial identification of who and what is in the room will then lead to the next step: setting achievable, short-term goals.

When engaging the task of building kingdom partnerships, here's a simple word of wisdom. Don't fall prey to the pressure to create anything. Look, rather, for what already has life, bless it, pray into it and track people and resources towards it. You can be sure those at the initial table will not "cover all the bases" of need in your city. Understand that you are establishing a "beachhead," a fresh initiative. For example, you may have on your team someone burdened to reach youth, another passionate about crisis pregnancy counseling, another keen on helping the poor or improving race relations. Typically, your team will be comprised predominantly of pastors and non-profit ministry leaders. In some cities, the movement may be led more by business and civic leaders. *Turn your team loose, expecting the Holy Spirit to oxygenate the embers and fires already burning in their hearts.* This approach has life, because the Lord is already in the equation, out ahead of us, waiting for leaders and everyday disciples to "get on his page, and get with his program" for touching and transforming individuals and institutions in your city.

5. Set Achievable, short-term goals.

Whether you're a formal team committed to implement a partnership, or a grassroots group of colleagues with a common passion for a local project, you're ready to assign specific roles and responsibilities. A colleague of mine calls this, "Getting the right people on the bus, and moving in the right direction." Do not fall prey to the tendency to "grab for the brass ring" in the short-term, to expend efforts going for a grandiose vision. Sure, with the presence and power of God in your equation, extraordinary, unexplainable things will and should be happening. I see two sides to a continuum. The first side, it is a good sign if you find yourself running to keep pace with divine activity! (C.S. Lewis, *The Chronicles of Narnia,* "Aslan is on the move!"). The second side, more pragmatic, is to set some achievable objectives and get some short-term wins. Keep your vision bar high enough to discern divine activity, at the same time being down to earth with what is achievable in the short term. You would be wise to get early wins. This typically means initiatives that can be accomplished in six to nine months.

6. Identify and publicize "entry ramps:" how to get involved

If you're reading this, you're already "on the train." You've rolled out of the station, you're down the tracks. But if you want to see more of God's kingdom assets actively partner in a concrete way in the fulfillment of your mission, you've got to provide some "handles on the train," ways in which people picking up pace alongside the tracks can grab onto what you're doing and go where God is taking you.

So, what is the most effective "handle," or "entry ramp?" Personal, face-to-face sharing of the vision, and recruitment, one at a time. If we cast a vision that is clear and compelling, and facilitate a process enlisting involvement, people will gladly sign up to partner in projects we promote. But such recruitment, in my experience, happens heart-to-heart. This kind of enlistment in a larger kingdom cause is neither taught nor bought, but caught. Clearly, the trend among millennial leaders is selective, spontaneous partnering based on both relational and missional resonance. As of this writing, this kind of non-structured spontaneity is on the rise.

A secondary means of recruitment for partnerships occurs in the context of a Forum, Focus Group or Roundtable where vision is cast, ideas and input are sought and opportunities for involvement explained. Also, someone may participate for the first time in a Serve Day, a Season of Service, backpack giveaway or Convoy of Hope, and get "hooked" on the joy of laboring alongside others to meet people's felt needs. And don't underestimate the increased effectiveness of social media, people sharing on facebook or twitter the joy of serving alongside folks from other churches meeting practical needs in their community.

7. Watch for a timely re-positioning of kingdom assets.

Here's an illustration. Walt and Kim re-located to our city from Portland. They were well established in that city, innovators of Alpha Group dinners for spiritual seekers, hands-on in numerous congregations. When Terri and I took them to lunch, they explained their move: "God began to stir our nest…then, on the same day, spoke to us independent of one another, 'I want you to move to Corvallis.'" Friends, you never know who might "parachute" into your movement next!

After that lunch, we briefed our local city team on the conversation. They gave us freedom to invite them both to step up and serve on the team, which they did. In five short years, this couple has become one of the most active kingdom assets in Corvallis. They purchased a bed and breakfast near the Oregon State University campus, and renovated it into "The Courtyard," a residence for Christian students. They provide the facility—meeting rooms, kitchen, coffee bar— free of charge for kingdom events and gatherings in our city. They also established a new non-profit, "Relevance," with a mission to communicate the gospel to seekers. Overall, on the city-reaching landscape, we're clearly in a season in which the Lord is re-positioning assets and putting his royal priesthood in place. I encourage you to pray and watch for fresh faces and fervent hearts to show up in *your* city!

Corroboration from a Secular Model

Collaboration among believing Christians has a spiritual component that brings the presence and glory of the Lord into the mix. But there is much to learn from secular models. Collaborative partnering can also have powerful results among good-hearted people who commit themselves to a shared cause. In 2012 an article was published in the *Stanford Social Innovation Review*.[1] I want to make a substantive, impressive article simple for our purposes. The authors identify five conditions that contribute to effective collaboration and that result in measurable social change. As we look at our cities, let's look not only at partnerships arising within the Body of Christ, but also at the potential of partnering with "men and women of peace," principled non-Christians with whom we may join to help remedy some of our most daunting social ills. Here are the bottom line conditions:

1. **A common agenda,** a shared vision for change. Any differences of mindset or approach are put on the table, discussed and resolved.

2. **Shared systems of measurement**, agreed upon means of quantifying outcomes.

3. **Regular activities that mutually reinforce the commitment** to the cause. Each stakeholder

commits to participation (in the collective impact model, these are CEO's, and not subordinates).

4. **Continuous communication:** taking time to create a common language and mutual trust is essential.

5. **"Backbone" support organizations** must be involved (at least one major, established organization that wields influence and monetary investment.

Here's a powerful, conclusive summary to this study: "The expectation that collaboration can occur without a supporting infrastructure is a frequent cause of failure." The parallels to what I've learned in the trenches over many years are clear. Here's the major takeaway for me from the study. If one or more "backbone" organizations get involved in a project, the measurable impact increases exponentially. The spending of both influence and monetary capital will pay great dividends. So, if the brightest, best and most philanthropic of secular players can see success with a model like this, then let's learn from them and create stunning models of God's royal priesthood partnering to release the redemptive presence and power of the kingdom throughout our communities.

Hindrances to Collaboration

Enlisting active partners to invest time, energy and resources in a new paradigm is challenging. In addition to natural and cultural obstacles, promoting unity and health in Christ's Body also attracts negative attention from the powers of darkness. God's Spirit promotes *integration* of each member of the "royal priesthood." The evil one promotes *dis-integration* through suspicion, mistrust, personality conflicts. If indeed God is giving us concrete answers to Jesus' priestly prayer for the witness of an organic oneness of his Body, we better take seriously Satan's threats to oppose and undermine these answers. It's no surprise, therefore, that Jesus also implores the Father, "Protect them from the power of the evil one" (Jo 17:11, 15). For a comprehensive understanding of the warfare, you would be wise to read Chapter 11 in the updated version of my book, *The Believers Guide to Spiritual Warfare*, and also Chapter 8 of this book.

Let me just touch on a few of the more obvious factors that can serve to inhibit the forging of functional, fruit-bearing partnerships. First, failure to communicate a clear, consistent and compelling vision will de-motivate the investment of prospective partners. Second, insufficient buy-in and ownership from a broad base of leaders of influence will limit the impact of your mission. Third, the challenge of bridging communication and collaboration among peoples of theological, generational and ethnic diversity can be daunting. While the *idea* of breaking these barriers is inspiring, the actual *implementation* can be disheartening! And fourth, a poor or non-existent strategy for funding the implementation of your mission may ultimately undermine the achievement of measurable outcomes. But while these are some common hindrances, let me address the one that can most typically sabotage the progress of your movement: strained relationships and unresolved conflict.

On the physical body, any wound that goes untended and untreated runs the risk of more serious infection. Even though resentment, envy, jealousy, criticism and strife are invisible attitudes, their affect on the spiritual Body of Christ are highly destructive. I have unpacked this issue quite extensively in *The Believers Guide to Spiritual Warfare*. It is sufficient to say here that if negative attitudes towards a brother or sister in your community go unresolved, the enemy may gain legal access, a "foothold" (Gr. topos, geographical place of influence), and work it to his advantage.

As we walk and work alongside those with different "wiring," there is always potential for friction. Irritation, annoyances and resentment are going to happen. If our hearts are sensitive to the Holy Spirit, and if we are quick to confess, the Lord covers us with forgiveness. But if we allow the attitude to fester, day after day, and we stonewall the Holy Spirit, a relationship can turn toxic. It becomes obsessive and oppressive, distracting and draining energy. In spiritual warfare terms, there is the danger that this hardness of heart escalates from foothold to stronghold. Paul gives us two clear "don'ts" in Ephesians 4: "don't grieve the Holy Spirit, and don't give the devil a foothold."

As you move forward trying to practice what "one church, many congregations" really looks like, as you get more intentional forging collaborative partnerships, give increased attention to resolving inter-personal conflicts, and closing a door on the devil. Break the destructive power of "cursing" (thinking and speaking negatively of someone) with the opposite spirit of "blessing," thinking and praying God's best for a brother or sister. While this blessing might run contrary to your emotions, choosing to bless and believe the best of another person releases God's favor, and shuts down enemy influence.

In summary, all kinds of hindrances and hassles are going to be a part of this turf. We are contending for increased impact of the life changing, resurrection power of Jesus Christ in our own backyards. Praise God we have increased numbers of healthy city movements in the US that are reaching the twenty and thirty year marks. We can only face and break through obstacles with Nehemiah-like leadership, calling on the project Manager in prayer at every turn, and walking in wisdom.

Sustaining and Maximizing Partnerships

Building enough trust to launch functional partnerships in a city is time and labor intensive. The endeavor calls for mature men and women at both leadership and grassroots levels to make sacrifices for a wider kingdom work, and for the common good of a city. That said, assuming the Lord's promise of the "commanded blessing" in Psalm 133 is true, we should expect and experience favor where his people choose to "dwell together in unity." So, once collaboration is "clicking" and producing results, what sustains motivation and energy to keep progress sustainable? I'd like to briefly touch on a few things that I think help energize on-going partnerships.

Enjoy the fellowship and the joy of co-laboring as colleagues.

If I might be down-to-earth, there is a genuine caring koinonia that I have seen in countless cities where the Psalm 133 commanded blessing is poured out. Clearly, Jesus regarded his disciples as "friends." Though we do not see evidence of natural humor and jesting, I'm certain he enjoyed the "guys and gals" he chose to walk and work with. And here's a piece from his walk in the vineyard with his disciples: "I have told you this so that my joy may be in you and that your joy may be complete" (Jo. 15:11). In short, to grab the title from a classic Michael Card song, there is "Joy in the Journey." Building a "koinonia culture" can grow deeper and sweeter year after year. This isn't Tom White *hype*. This is the blessed *hope* that fills the hearts of men and women who choose to dwell together.

In the early years working with the leaders of Skopje, Macedonia, I showed up with my Western agenda, a pack of talking points, and geared up for a serious meeting. Well, the coffee, crackers and cheese hit the table, the jokes started (in Macedonian, of course!), laughter erupted, and I was… frustrated! Until I learned that this was *their* way of sharing Jesus' joy with one another. The simplicity of just being together *was* more of the "agenda" than my action points. The love and joy of Jesus Christ filling and spilling out of human hearts engaged in common mission is contagious. This kind of supernatural empowerment will sustain purposeful partnerships through thick and thin.

Share stories and surprises.

Generally speaking, Christians presume on one another. We just expect others to show up and put up to advance our witness of oneness, and any particular partnership we're committed to. Sure, everyone understands that sacrificial investment of time, energy, expertise and resources is a part of the work. But I believe that partnerships work, and keep working, when we take the initiative to affirm another's unique contribution. This may be as simple as a "thank you," or as meaningful as publicly acknowledging the value of someone's service. Here's a word from Paul that applies here: "Do not let any unwholesome talk come out of your mouths, but only what is helpful for building others up according to their needs, that it may benefit those who listen" (Eph. 4:29). Appreciation edifies, blesses and releases supernatural energy that keeps faithful workers in the game.

Look for infusions of new people and fresh ideas

I like this word "infusion," the receiving of life-giving vitality. For any leadership team, as hard as we try not to, we will predictably get into our own heads, our own patterns of "group think," our own understanding of what the movement is or should be. And, as hard as we may try to communicate, and be approachable for new inputs and ideas, there is always a danger that an existing team becomes the "in group," becoming both stale and self-perpetuating. So, keep your leadership fluid. Keep the door open for fresh troops, new ideas. In the next Chapter, I'll talk more specifically about the current transfer of leadership from Boomer to Gen-Ex and Millennial leaders.

And finally, in the on-going effort to keep leadership fluid and effective, keep a balance of familiar and fresh. By familiar, I mean a core of leaders who were involved birthing the movement (innovators, pioneers) or who showed up in the early stages (early adopters). By fresh I mean emerging leaders, ethnic leaders with a different, "non-white" grid, and late adopters who have recently discovered your mission. The best analogy here is a relay race, with a variety of runners, with distinctive skills and speeds working together. As one runner rounds his last lap, the next runner is already moving, hand extended, running alongside his teammate until the baton is safely passed, and firmly gripped. This is partnership. *I strongly believe this expression of the "city church" can perk along for decades, sustained by the joy of a koinonia culture, the grace gifts of the Holy Spirit, and leaders who have learned when to lean in, and when to let go. Why not? Why not you? Why not your community?*

Re-claiming the King's City: The "Rest of the Story"

In any endeavor, nothing speaks louder than on-the-ground reality. I realize there are many models of "city transformation" we could look at, all "works in progress." I want to close with a story about kingdom partnering that brings promise, and stirs hope. In Chapter 4, I shared the story of a dramatic shift in city leadership that I helped facilitate in Kingston, Ontario in 2006. The "King's Town" is, I believe, on the innovative edge of the city transformation paradigm in Canada. Here's the "rest of the story."

In the spring of 2010, I helped the small core team of the Kingston Transformation Network select candidates who would stand for election to an expanded leadership team to serve this institutional city (hospitals, schools, government, prisons). There were at least two prospects in each of these categories: pastors, non-profit ministries, marketplace leaders, emerging leaders, intercessors and serving ministries. While there was some apprehension about "voting," the selection came off without a hitch. A team of fourteen individuals was appointed. Roger Rutter, business owner and point man, commented to me the next day, before I left town, "Well, now I've got a pack of wild horses. What do you suggest I *do* with them?" I advised Roger to go slow, and spend the summer getting to know one another better in more informal settings, and work with his wife Bonnie discerning each person's core passion. Then, I booked in an overnight team retreat with them for October.

At the retreat, each person unpacked his or her passion. David, a retired Anglican pastor, took responsibility for leading a weekly prayer time for kingdom leaders. Will and Catherine, regional leaders for the Salvation Army, took point planning a spring consortium on biblical justice. Maria, business owner and head of Kingston's Chamber of Commerce, got excited about communications, and sharing KTN's mission with other business leaders. Jeff, a mortgage broker in his early 30's, was stirred to connect with the Mayor's Special Commission on Homelessness and Affordable Housing. Roger was keen to serve as a liaison to Bridgeway Homes, a non-profit that places foster children in Christian homes. He also took responsibility to begin negotiations with the city government renting the Sports Arena for five years for "Kingdom Come," an annual citywide gathering for worship and prayer. Suddenly, overnight, this diverse "pack of wild horses" was up and running, each in their own track, at their own pace, free to recruit others of like mind and heart around their passion. A fresh, pliable wineskin of kingdom leadership was in place with "entry ramps" identified for others to get involved in a sustainable endeavor to be salt and light for the city, the Province, and the nation. These men and women, a mix of church and marketplace leaders, are faithfully stewarding a contextual expression of the Royal Priesthood, finding creative ways to partner in sharing the good news and doing good works, "so that (Kingston) will believe" (John 17:21).

Understand, this group had history. Roger and Bonnie had for ten years prior led a core group of seasoned intercessors every Thursday night praying in the Council Chambers in City Hall. Two years after the first KTN team was appointed, Roger gave leadership to a citywide outreach, Impact World Tour, getting entrée into most of the schools for born-again skateboarders and athletes, concluding the week with an outreach in the K-Rock Center. Everyone that got involved loved the cooperation, the synergy of working together on something that released blessing to the city. Roger had been faithful to lead a trustworthy process and to enlist a wide diversity of people to partner together.

In reality, some of the partnerships in Kingston are strong, getting traction, taking off. Others are lagging. Also, there are still many pastors and congregations not buying in. There are many of the "royal priesthood" planted in the marketplace that have yet to find their place on the wall. This all takes time, but with leadership, covered and empowered by intercession, functional partnerships that steward kingdom influence grow and bear fruit.

Summing up, I believe we are just beginning to release God's "royal priesthood" in our cities. Around two years ago my word of the year was "traction." City movements began getting "unstuck." Many began reporting signs of momentum. We're beginning to see the tangible results of this "anointed activism" I spoke of earlier, the "long obedience in the same direction." When collaborative kingdom partnerships are birthed out of a commonly shared love for Jesus Christ, and anointed by the power of the Holy Spirit, partnering together to share good news and do good deeds becomes a journey that is joyous, bearing lasting fruit to the glory of our King.

Chapter Seven

Looking Out Ahead: Trends in the City Transformation Paradigm

Trying to identify trends in a bona fide "movement" is risky. In view of the fast pace of change occurring in our culture, even a reasonably good read on the future will quickly be outdated. Given the mind-boggling advances in communication technology, we are experiencing a rapidity and complexity of change that is, frankly, dizzying. So, I realize the risk of producing a "trends" chapter. But as a veteran city movement practitioner, I also see the value of putting an eye to the growth curve, and inquire, "what's next?" I'll give you my best shot, and then watch for either accolades or dismissal as the years roll by, probably a healthy balance of both.

To spread the opinion curve a bit, I have just concluded fascinating conversations with seven colleagues, innovative world changers engaged in a diversity of cultures, asking: *"What trends are you observing? Where do you see?* the Holy Spirit taking this movement?"

There are three things I'd like to share up front. First, any endeavors to continue to build increased health of relationships in Christ's Body, corporate prayer and missional collaboration in specific venues is undeniably biblical and worthy of our efforts. Why? Because Jesus said so explicitly in his last conversation with his disciples (John 15-16), and in his prayer to the Father recorded in John 17. In my view, promoting oneness of heart and mission in a city or neighborhood will be a God-honoring investment, until the end of time. Jesus commands his followers to walk and work together in covenantal love. So, being engaged building local expressions of kingdom community has a foundation of core values and orthodox doctrine that will not change. Jesus, our cornerstone, and the teachings of the apostles and prophets, are that *foundation* (Eph. 2:19-22).

But change in culture brings with it a call for fresh *adaptation,* adjusting our practice of community to be more understandable and accessible to the current cultural milieu. Visionary leaders must therefore not simply be open to such change, but rather anticipate it and embrace it. The integrity of our core biblical theology must remain strong and cohesive. But signposts that give directions and entry ramps that give access to such kingdom communities must connect relevantly with current culture.

Second, let's be up front about our Western propensity to identify working components, plan and predict outcomes. We may think we've got this "city movement thing" figured out, but truth be known, it's the hand of God that touches and changes people and places for the better. So, don't hear

Looking Out Ahead: Trends in the City Transformation Paradigm

me wrong. I'm all for "anointed activism," moving in sync with God's Spirit to advance kingdom influence. So, if sovereign God is inspiring and empowering our plans and projects, we go for it. But here's the word of wisdom: let's submit our propensities for planning to Christ's Lordship, and be careful to inquire of him before we act on our highest and most noble endeavors.

And third, I have learned that the "big idea" of getting everyone in a large, complex city on the same page doing one strategy is just that…a "big idea." In any given city there will be a diversity of players engaged in kingdom work. *In my view, we need to celebrate the creativity and spontaneity of God's Spirit calling a variety of people to work on such intractable problems like the homeless issue, affordable housing, human trafficking, placing children in foster care, etc.* Such multiplicity and diversity of kingdom-centered initiatives is healthy. Watch for where the Spirit is working, who is working with him, and bring your passion, calling, gifts and skillsets to that mix.

Trend #1:
Ownership and Engagement of the "Early Majority"

Most of us are familiar with the bell curve that depicts the birth and development of movements. At the front end, there are a small number of pioneers, innovators, "early adopters." As a movement gains life and momentum, others discover it and sign on. This group, larger in size, comprises "late adopters." Around the top of the curve we find the emergence of the "early majority," existing leaders or organizations that bring with them an increase of influence and resources. Suddenly it seems like the institutional players "see it and get it." They discover the legitimacy of the ideas and energy behind an authentic movement. And while the original innovators are glad to see this development, it also presents a new set of challenges. Having paid a high price of time, energy and scant resources to get something "out of the gate," suddenly major players start talking the same language, and spending their influence capital to shape the paradigm. This is a welcome change, with many new players, but this transition has its adjustments. We just need to keep relationship and honest communication at the core of all we do.

Well, this is currently the case in the city transformation movement. In September, 2010, the key leaders of the New York City Leadership Center launched "Movement Day," inviting practitioners of city movements, leaders of national evangelical non-profits, and leaders in the New York city area. Plenary speakers included Dr. Tim Keller and Bill Hybels. At Movement Day 2012, Tim Keller and the father-son team of Luis and Kevin Palau brought plenary messages. I believe the work of the Holy Spirit in the context of cities is now being showcased. This is a very good development. The major movers and shakers of American evangelicalism (the "early majority") have discovered what veteran city-reachers have been up to for thirty years: real people in a real place being real serious about walking and working in unity to grow God's kingdom. So, what we have is a positively new wineskin, a mix of veterans and early majority taking the movement to a whole new place.

Looking Out Ahead: Trends in the City Transformation Paradigm

In this regard, I got very excited recently reading MOVE, the results of the Willow Creek "Reveal" study, "What 1,000 Churches Reveal About Spiritual Growth." Chapter 15, "Pastor the Local Community," poses this question: What if a number of healthy, disciple-making congregations get a vision for working together to more effectively shepherd their city? "That's it!" I shouted to myself, another entry ramp for catalyzing a city-reaching movement. Willow has clearly "caught" what on-the-ground practitioners have affirmed for years: "Best practice pastors see a natural affinity between evangelizing and serving those who are struggling and broken—because people who feel hopeless have hearts that are fertile ground for Christ's message of grace and redemption". [1]

Jim Herrington, one of the co-founders of the Mission Houston movement, concurs that we are now in the "early majority" stage of the bell curve. He feels we now need to work at bringing people at all stages of the movement into collaboration: innovators, early and mid-stage adopters, and now the early majority. In Jim's perspective, it is time to provide practical training, conferences, workshops where we better understand the skill-sets needed to advance movements, and the how-to's of implementation.

Let me share a few concerns about the arrival of the "early majority." There are clear upsides, with added weight and momentum from individuals of influence, administrative staff, and monetary resources. But let's be honest about the potential downsides, the propensity of Western Christianity to organize, publicize and monetize the "next new thing." We all need to stay close to Jesus' heart here, guarding against our default mode of offering him our "best stuff." The best of our influence, mission statements, gifting and budgeting will not advance his kingdom. We must stay ever sensitive to the Holy Spirit as we steward the grace deposit we've received. We must realize that the momentum that marks a true movement can go off the rails at any point, misguided by human ambition, even our own best intentions. This is a delicate "dance." This is what I mean by "anointed activism." As long as there are wise leaders among us who understand that we cannot humanly catalyze and sustain authentic supernatural transformation, but rather steward it in the grace of God, the gospel movement wineskin can be poised to bear increased, lasting fruit.

Trend #2:
Transfer of Leadership from Existing to Emerging Leaders

We are well down the road of a changeover to the postmodernist mindset. Frankly, America seems to be sprinting towards a predominant post-Christian culture. While the post-World War II "boomer" generation has labored hard building organizations, designing and launching projects and managing strategies, the world as we have known it has changed. The emerging generation of leaders is not keen on meetings. "Program" sounds to them like a four-letter word. Even the mention of "training" gets little traction. Emerging leaders lean towards tolerance over hard-and-fast truth, treasure raw transparency over touting religious platitudes, and believe actions speak louder than words. In one very meaningful chat I caught with a young leader, he said this: "We're not necessarily wanting you guys to get behind what we're doing, or how we're doing it. We just want you to get behind *us*." Here it is again, family language, fathers encouraging and imparting life to their sons.

But there is also a keen priority of mission that is in play here. Recently, in a city where I coach, a group of existing leaders, the patriarchal founders of the movement, engaged the emerging leaders in some honest dialogue. One young church planter spoke up: "While I respect who you guys are, and what you've built, it seems to me like you've got the cart before the horse. Your 'horse' is unity of relationships, being friends, praying together, etc., and you pull along a 'cart' of events and missional stuff. I think the 'horse' should be God's mission, behind which we align and engage our collaborative energies." There is a clear shift in perspective here. Less meetings, more mission. Less prayer, more pro-active engagement meeting practical needs. In the mind of Millenials, relationships find meaning and purpose through engaging in life-on-life justice issues or in the trenches mingling with unbelievers.

In many movements, this generational transfer of power is actually coming off quite well. I "get" the aversion to the values, styles and structures propagated by the boomer and builder generations. The critique hits home. And it is leading to some healthy adjustments in how we partner in multi-generational kingdom work.

In April 2012 I had a meal with a core group of leaders serving with "Love Ottawa," Canada. There was a new face at the table, Dave, pastor of a missional community in the urban core. I asked, "If business as usual keeps going on with this team, with monthly meetings, slick communication pieces and occasional projects, will you and others your age participate in leadership?" He responded quickly: "No, we don't do long meetings and projects." What Dave and his wife *really* do is to engage life in the urban core, and invite local residents/seekers to share meals with them, engage in conversations, and, when appropriate, invite them to a Bible study. One by one, these local "friends" are opening their lives to Jesus.

In 2008 I was invited to speak at the biannual Transforum Conference of "Together for Berlin," what I consider to be the best organized and defined city movement in Europe. It all began in 2001 with prayer and relationship building between pastors. Recently, I checked in with Axel, Nehlsen patriarch and point man. I was thrilled to hear about the changes. For ten years Axel and his colleagues had been intentional bringing the influence of the gospel into all of the spheres ("domains") in greater Berlin, the "big vision" as he called it. "But now we've become more of an open network that seeks to connect other movements at the grassroots level of neighborhoods. We find where the Spirit is moving, pray over the work, and resource it if we can."

They recently completed a survey seeking to identify how many missional movements have been launched in Berlin in the last ten years. They documented over eighty initiatives, mostly small neighborhood-specific endeavors focused on serving and outreach, e.g., cafes for drug-addicted prostitutes, coffee houses for Muslims, and church plants reaching out to neighborhoods. In an area with very little church presence, someone planted a congregation in a high-rise apartment complex, also raising funds for a family cafeteria and a playground. Church members are also trained in marriage and family counseling. In another needy neighborhood, a group from Switzerland showed up, bought a vacant church building, and planted a monastary ("cloister"), with regular services and retreats.

Axel was explicit: "We just had to adjust to the post-modern milieu here, and change our top-down thinking to encourage multi-centric, de-centralized connections based on relationship and missional passion." They did another questionnaire targeting kingdom leaders under thirty-five. Here are three of the results: 1) We appreciate that Together for Berlin organizes things and creates the space for connections, 2) we don't want regular organizational meetings, and we don't want an agenda; let's meet three times a year to talk about what God is doing in our hearts and neighborhoods, and 3) we don't want to participate in a regular prayer meeting. Here is Axel's summary: *"These people don't want to be members of another organization, but rather part of something organic that generates life."*

Yes, the Together for Berlin city leadership team remains functional with a flat hierarchy at multiples levels, meeting monthly, or less. But what is fresh and bearing the most fruit is the "Spiritual Advisory Network," more of a relationship-based group of thirty leaders who meet three times a year for one day for lively, open exchange of ideas, and to pray for one another and the city. There is a clear delineation of particular passions, women's issues, broken families, human trafficking, ethnic churches, etc. Here's the chief role of the Together for Berlin leadership team: encourage these organic connections, pray for their endeavors, and resource them. What I mostly heard in Axel's voice was excitement, an enthusiasm about the spontaneity of life being birthed and sustained by the Spirit of God. And an additional encouraging factor: the Berlin team is now intentionally connecting with the Emmanuel Gospel Center team in Boston, developing a leadership learning community. There is an increased trend for leaders of cities of comparable size and cultural complexity to connect, share and compare stories, and learn from one another. Axel's colleagues have also catalyzed another twelve *"Together For Berlin"* initiatives in other parts of Germany. Such replication is a great sign of authentic kingdom life!

It's a long way in distance and culture from Germany to "down under" in Australia. I re-connected recently with Ian Shelton, longtime pastor of the Toowoomba City Church in Toowoomba (100 kilometers west of Brisbane), and a dedicated innovator of Body unity in cities since the mid-1970's. His inputs confirmed what I see the Spirit doing in other parts of the world. Ian has sown his life into unity of the Body of Christ, not only throughout Australia, but also New Zealand, Fiji, and Papua New Guinea. He shared some fresh developments in Toowoomba:

1. They are seeking to discern a corporate kingdom strategy for Toowoomba that focuses on renewal of the church and a release of God's shalom to

their city in greater measure. This involves a mix of local pastors, non-profits and business leaders, who seek the Lord regularly to envision together how to release greater favor from the Father.

2. In addition to Ian and his wife Betty, four other pastors and their wives have transitioned to serve the city movement as "leaders emeritus." The Lord has raised up Andrew, a forty-one year old professor of bio-medicine, father of eight, with a ministry of healing and deliverance (in his spare time!). Andrew is so known and respected in the community, he has picked up the reins of leadership. Here are a few of their fresh initiatives:

   -- Calling young pastors and business leaders to step up to serve the city vision

   -- "City Women" stepping up to fight the sexualization of the culture

   -- Receiving increased donations from secular businesses to target social needs (people of good faith partnering with people of good will to engage in good deeds)

   -- Planting new churches, with increased conversions and baptisms

3. Ian has just re-ignited a nation-wide communication piece, "One Heart for the Nation," and put it on-line (www.oneheart.com.au). With an incurable passion for John 17 unity, Ian seems to be in constant motion connecting with other

city movements in Australia and beyond, sharing stories of cities getting breakthrough in unity and supernatural transformation.

The passing of the leadership mantle in city movements is well underway. Frankly, with all of our human foibles and failings, we need to do our best getting this right. As existing leaders, let's be faithful to steward this transition, staying at the helm as long as needed, encouraging and cheering emerging leaders on. And my challenge to emerging leaders: step up, speak up, show up. With relay baton in hand, look forward, focus, and run! In Corvallis, we're in process discerning how to get this relay hand-off thing right. Recently, sitting with three key, emerging senior pastor leaders in our city, I shared this word, on behalf of our existing city leadership team: "We want to give you guys the space to have your own conversations, and to envision what the future looks like in our city. We pray God's grace to cover and empower your efforts, and we release you to find your own pace as you pick this up, and walk it out." As I glanced at my colleagues, fellow stewards of a movement two decades in the making, it was clear to me that the responsibility for the race, and the strength of *our* pace, was gearing down. And I could also clearly hear fresh footsteps on the track, and see hands reaching out to take the baton. I'm already savoring the satisfaction of slipping into the role of "track star emeritus!"

Trend #3:
Cross-Sector Partnership and Collaboration

A trend well underway and getting traction in many cities is "cross sector collaboration." There is a synergy here, a blending of skill-sets and sharing of resources when leaders of influence join hearts and hands from the major sectors: Public (government, military, education, medicine), Private (business, arts and media) and Social (faith community, non-profits and families). Following on from a Luis Palau Festival in 2010, and mobilizing hundreds of churches and thousands of believers in a "season of service," the Vision San Diego leadership team is now taking point to engage leaders of influence from the public and private sectors to improve the educational system in San Diego County. *Without compromising core truths of the gospel that define who we are, it is time to be salt and light in the seedy and needy places of our cities.*

Tim Svoboda, urban specialist with YWAM ministered in Chennai, India for twenty years, serving on the initial Chennai Transformation Network leadership team. With San Francisco now his home base, Tim talks about "faithfulness, not formulas" in reaching a city, men and women sowing their lives into defined neighborhoods. In Tim's view, the organized efforts of structural citywide movements are not getting much traction, but consortiums of churches and non-profits engaged in specific neighborhoods are. He is tracking the "parish collective" movement, seeking to bring incarnational presence: real people, engaging in real places, and engaging their passions (suicide prevention, domestic violence, human trafficking, homelessness).

Tim was most impressed with one pastor's passion to touch his "parish," a twelve block area in a nearly one hundred percent gay neighborhood. He is not interested in meetings or strategies. His aim is to shepherd the souls in his "parish." He recently offered a "Jesus Workshop," sharing his understanding of the gospel story. So, the takeaway from Tim's involvement with city endeavors over thirty years: the power and potential for transformational change happens in individual hearts at the grassroots, with "micro-focused apostles" caring and praying their way into needy hearts.

George Ordway, Founder of Communities, Inc. in Fresno, CA, has been a participant in a rare collaboration that is not only cross-sector, but cross racial. The West Fresno Ministerial Alliance (WFMA), the oldest and predominantly black association of ministers, has welcomed integration with other racial spheres in the city, even to the point of racially integrated prayer meetings. Similarly, the Coalition of Hispanics in the Valley (CHEV), in George's words, "is alive and well reaching across racial and denominational lines to advance the gospel mission throughout California's Central Valley.

Trend #4:
City Movements are Maturing

We're familiar with the Chinese proverb: "the journey of a thousand miles begins with a single step. Men and women with grit and determination have been at this over thirty years. We can now confidently say there are "lights on a hill," modern day Antiochs and Thessalonicas that trumpet the glory of God dwelling in increased measure in the midst of his people:. the thirty year plus journey of Fresno, which traces its origin to the famous "no name fellowship," the impressive story of Mission Houston, the sustainable

Nehemiah Network in Little Rock, the healthy inter-racial Tuscaloosa Prayer Network, the emerging prospect of multi-sector collaboration of Vision San Diego, the launching of "Movement Day" by the New York City Leadership Center in 2010.

In brief, I can say at this point on the path, "This wineskin is working!" So, for some movements that have been on this journey for two to three decades, here are some signs of increased maturity.

1. **Peer-to-peer mentoring and coaching.**

Increasingly, I see purposeful connections occurring between city movements, catalyzed predominantly through close relationships. This is at the heart of the Berlin-Boston relationship. As a part of the "Movement Day" journey, the leadership teams of ten large US cities made a covenant in 2010 to walk together for five years, sharing case studies and best practices. Also in the context of Movement Day, my associate Glenn Barth (Good Cities) and George Ordway (Communities, INC) designed and pioneered a two day "City Advance," a leadership learning community model for city team cohort groups, engaging relevant issues, and discerning fresh action steps. *We are clearly at a point where we need less new information, and increased impartation of the power of the Holy Spirit that leads to implementation.*

2. **Increased partnering of people of good faith and good will.**

As social and economic problems of our cities and culture increase in both complexity and quantity, we need to engage the cross sector collaboration I spoke of earlier, partnering with both Christian and non-Christian leaders of good will from the private, public and social sectors. We're just "on the cusp" of this development. Of course we need to hold firm to core biblical orthodoxy, but be unafraid to work with non-Christian men and women who have passion for the same issues we care about. In their brilliant work *To Transform a City*, Eric Swanson and Sam Williams talk about engaging with people of good will on "centered set" issues, areas of cohesion around finding solutions to common social ills. The "bounded set" mentality is exclusive: "You don't agree with my theology or methodology. therefore I won't work with you." Centered set thinking opens a door to collaborate inclusively with a variety of players in a city seeking answers to daunting, systemic issues.

3. A movement in the West partnering with an international movement.

At Oregon's "Church of the Valley" Prayer Summit in February, 2012, I was brought into a very stimulating conversation, with a "what if" question. I anticipate this same question and dialogue are emerging in many city movements coming into maturity, as they increasingly look outward. What if our movement could partner with another city movement overseas to work collaboratively to bring the gospel to an unreached people group? This is an incredibly "big idea" in search of a bold innovator, or, more likely, a group of bold innovators working together in the context of a city movement. Might we be an Antioch city, training and preparing to send out ambassadors of good deeds and good news to turn on the light of the gospel in a dark corner of the world?

Looking Out Ahead: Trends in the City Transformation Paradigm

Anyone who understands cross-cultural mission knows the folly of thinking a Western Christian organization, or city movement, can "parachute" into a radically different culture and "reach" it in any measurable way in the short term. But what I'm envisioning here is a healthy movement in the West, where a culture of John 17 oneness, corporate prayer and missional obedience has been stewarded well, undergirding a movement of similar kingdom "dna" that is in proximity to unreached peoples. Could it not be on God's heart for an established movement to encourage, pray for, resource and train those in another city to more effectively incarnate Jesus' life giving message to a people still bound in unbelief by the powers of darkness? I'm convinced this is on God's radar, and we'll soon begin to see these trans-local, trans-cultural connections coming on-line.

4. Disaster readiness and response.

As a movement matures and grows to become more "other oriented," preparations are often put in place to respond more quickly and effectively to crisis and disaster. This was the case with the massive flood that hit Cedar Rapids, Iowa. Charles Daugherty, Director of Serve the City, mobilized his citywide networks at the height of the floods, and to this day is still engaged meeting on-going needs. In August, 2005, after Hurricane Katrina ripped into the Gulf Coast, the Tuscaloosa Prayer Network found itself mobilizing to provide shelter, food and clothing for over a thousand refugees. And in April, 2010, several neighborhoods in Tuscaloosa were devastated by tornados. Again, God's people rose to the moment, and are still active in the trenches helping many re-build their shattered lives. In October, 2012, several core leaders from the Tuscaloosa movement trekked up to New Jersey and

New York to help the victims of super storm Sandy, with tool belts, food and resources in hand.

As I write this chapter, the F-5 tornado has devastated Moore, OK. God may call any city movement at any time to step up and respond to a natural calamity, economic collapse, a serial shooter going off the tracks, or a terrorist threat. I believe we're seeing the emergence of "cities of refuge," places and peoples uniquely prepared by God to be places to which people in stress can come, and from which kingdom ambassadors can go to bring help and hope to those facing calamities of all sorts. The Christian Emergency Network is a great resource for training and preparation along these lines (www.christianemergencynetwork.org).

5. Entrepreneurship and job creation.

I believe creative, "out of the box" thinking qualifies as a mark of maturity of a gospel movement, stepping back from the typical conversations and concerns leaders carry for a city. Under the leading of the Holy Spirit, with the release of his creativity, might there be a unique opening for intellectual and business entrepreneurs in the Body of Christ to create new companies, spawn micro-finance and micro-business endeavors? The Hebrew notion of "shalom" describes all-encompassing blessing, sovereign God pouring out favor that is inclusive of spiritual, emotional and physical blessing. In our cities, we are well accustomed to leaders who bring us spiritual inspiration, and quality instruction. Let's also be on the lookout for leaders who will bring practical innovation.

One of the measurable indicators of the spiritual transformation of a city is the increase of commerce, the opening of job opportunities. In gospel movements growing toward maturity, I would recommend open forums where innovative thinkers could share ideas on how and where Christians with means could launch new business endeavors, develop new products or provide unique services. One distinct sign of the season we are now in is a breaking down of the dichotomy between sacred and secular spheres (church and business), and between pastors and marketplace leaders. If indeed we are God's chosen, and planted in specific places, might we not take our role as a "royal priesthood" seriously and minister to the peoples of our cities the balance of good news, and good deeds? The opportunity to labor, and enjoy the satisfaction and product of our work is a core contributor to human dignity.

Trend #5:
Leading with the Gospel.

There is a familiar maxim gaining momentum in the circles of city transformation practitioners: the doing of good works among unbelievers will foster increased good will, soften hearts, and open spontaneous opportunities to share the good news. Gladly, over the past decade, on the continuum that balances good works and good news (biblical justice and evangelism), the pendulum among traditional evangelicals has swung back towards good deeds, service, caring for people's here-and-now needs. But while this is a welcome swing, there is fresh "chatter" in the city-reaching ranks: our faithful, loving service is not yet reaping much of a measurable increase of souls coming into the kingdom.

Like others, I'm doing my best to navigate my way through post-modern culture, where tolerance for everyone's unique story seems elevated above objective truth. I have come to a conviction that I am to walk in the Spirit and engage a lifestyle witness of praying for unbelievers in my world, taking time to care for them through active listening, watching for the Holy Spirit to open opportunities to share my personal story, with an aim to relate it to the bigger story of the good news.

In his closing plenary at Movement Day 2012, Tim Keller shared what he felt must be some of the distinctives of a vibrant citywide Church. Two of these distinctives: "the Church must be a contrast community, and a prophetic community." This hit home. With all of our efforts to do good deeds, and serve people's needs, we have to be careful to not just be about winning not-yet-believers to just like us more (doing good deeds so we'll be seen and accepted as "good guys"), but to Jesus, and his offer of eternal life. *The bottom line, we have to be unapologetic and unafraid proclaiming unvarnished truth that confronts people with a decision to repent and follow Jesus Christ.*

In July, 2012, Rice Broocks, Director of Every Nation Ministries, published a timely article in Charisma magazine. Noting a renewed interest in the gospel, and increased numbers of testimonies of conversions, Rice shares that "Christian ministries seem to be awakening from a long season of evangelistic futility." He references the results of research done by Ed Stetzer of LifeWay, that a scant 3% of churches in North America are growing through conversion growth. If anywhere near accurate, this statistic is dismal. But Brooks is optimistic:

> "This new movement could be described as the beginning of an 'evangelistic spring' in North America. Signs of a fresh boldness in Christian witnessing are popping up everywhere…make no mistake, though. The snow has not fully melted yet from this long winter of meager evangelistic growth in the West." [2]

Rice's most recent book, *God's Not Dead,* re-visits many of the classic apologetic themes, but with a distinct postmodern flavor.

While we're all familiar with numerous conversation starters like this, we often have a failure of nerve moving out of our cultural comfort zones to engage people with truth. I believe one of the clear upsides of cultivating a city gospel movement is a commitment to build a culture of kingdom leaders accountable to one another for praying fervently and expectantly for the lost, doing good deeds caring for real felt needs, all the while watching for the Holy Spirit to open doors for sharing the good news.

I love this quote I picked up listening to Steve Sjogren talking about the simplicity of praying our way into people's hearts:"This is all about everyday people demonstrating and declaring the gospel in car pools, on the sidelines of a soccer match, around water coolers." Author of *Conspiracy of Kindness and 101 Ways to Reach Your City,* Steve's winsome approach is down-to-earth:"As you pray for others, 'noticing' what God is doing in their lives, you allow God to point out needs as well as opportunities. It's as if he is 'noticing' through you."[3] Recognizing that most of us get nervous about sharing our faith, he encourages us to be creative showing kindness. We don't need to be pushy or obnoxious, just "notice" how the Holy Spirit might be working in someone's mind and heart. I love how Steve describes these encounters:

> "Instead of blasting away, do some 'story listening.' That can turn into 'story exchanging,' which leads to the best gospel story-telling. Many avoid evangelism because it usually puts pressure on those who speak and those who listen. It gets clouded with fear and guilt on both sides...Even small bits of banter with people can unfold into some amazing conversations."[4]

So, what's the trend? To be comfortable and more intentional noticing, caring and praying our way into the minds and hearts of the spiritually lost, in obedience to the creative leadings of the Holy Spirit. To steward in our cities an on-going culture of praying and caring for, and sharing the good news with people. I predict we will see many new expressions of incarnational witness coming on-line, creative, ways of gently but intentionally pointing seekers towards the greatest story ever told.

Trend #6:
Training/Employing Catalytic Leaders to Serve Emerging Movements.

I have always found surfing videos exhilarating, intrigued by the courage and competence it really takes to maneuver a

Looking Out Ahead: Trends in the City Transformation Paradigm

massive mountain of water. In October, 2011, I checked off a box on my bucket list, taking a surfing lesson on Maui. It was enough for me to size up my first set of three to four foot waves! By God's grace, and a small mix of athleticism, I got up on my first wave. Well, after getting out through the surf five or six times, and resting before the next catch, I began noticing a few things, like where the waves were coming from, cycles of when the larger ones built up, what size they might be, and, most of all, how to begin to posture myself to engage a decent wave, minimize energy, and maximize the force of nature with a good ride.

If catalyzing gospel movements in cities and regions is a "wave" rising, then how might we better anticipate the wave and posture ourselves to move with it? How might we be working to prepare a new cadre of surfing instructors, giving men and women skills to help birth and develop John 17 kingdom communities? In my observations of Trend #1, Jim Herrington affirmed that the "early majority" of evangelicalism in North America is now showing up, and with that development, we should be looking to provide increased training opportunities for those called to steward transformational movements.

When Mac Pier first recruited me to serve on the Leadership Cabinet of "Movement Day," I recall him sharing a phrase that has remained in my "idea inbox." He talked about the urgent need to provide a "leadership pipeline," equipping the next generation of leaders called and better equipped to catalyze sustainable gospel movements in the city context. For ten years, I served as one of four Conveners of the National City Impact Roundtable, an annual "big tent" gathering of practitioners from cities of different size and complexity, sharing stories, best practices and getting fresh ideas from plenary speakers. As I write, I am currently engaged with colleagues Glenn Barth (Good Cities) and George Ordway (Communities, Inc.) designing a third year model for "City Advance," a pre-Movement Day leadership learning community for cohort groups of leaders from established movements.

In the Spring of 2012, I began developing a core of training materials for a new educational module, "CitiCoach," designed for men and women involved hands-on in their own movement, but also with a call to catalyze gospel movements trans-locally in other places. At this stage of my journey, I'm taking seriously Paul's admonition to Timothy, to "entrust (incarnational truth) to reliable men who will also be qualified to teach others" (2 Tim. 2:2). Such training must not simply be didactic, imparting principles and a list of best practices. This has to be an on-the-job apprenticeship training, learning by doing, de-briefing mistakes, celebrating breakthroughs. This is a cutting edge priority for the next ten years of my calling and journey.

Let me share a few samples of learning/training opportunities already on the gospel movement radar: www.cityreaching.com (this site has been around the longest, with numerous resources available) www.oneheart.com (launched in August, 2012, networking city movements in Australia be South Pacific), and www.gospelmovements.com (managed by the Luis Palau Association), and Doxa Deo, the movement in

Pretoria, South Africa (www.doxadeo.co.za). I'm very impressed with a model pioneered by Jim Herrington in Houston aimed at making disciples in the context of the marketplace (www.faithwalking.us).

Building City Cultures that Bear Lasting Fruit

So, some of these trends might play out, hopefully pan out, in some measure. For sure there will be others that show up that I have not anticipated in these pages. But *I want to return to this question: What are we really after, what are we hoping to see result from all this activity in our cities?* I believe Jesus' words to his disciples in the Upper Room is the best we will find. The Father is clear on wanting "fruit that will last" (John 15:16), lives transformed by his grace, names written in the book of life, the making and shaping of kingdom disciples. And all of this, so he will receive the glory he is due. Isaiah 61:1-3, the ministry of Messiah, also answers the question: preaching good news, healing broken hearts, setting captives free, and planting oaks of righteousness…"for the display of his splendor." Jesus calls his disciples to partner with him, the Father and the Spirit in bringing forth an abundance of fruit.

Personally, as I ponder trends from an American perspective, I do not see a national, sweeping awakening on the horizon. If that comes, I welcome it, and will help sustain it. But what I clearly see are men and women in cities taking seriously their responsibility to steward the building of kingdom covenantal communities. I see believers looking beyond the walls of their church, seeing the pain of their city, and praying, "Lord, break my heart over the things that break your heart." As I close a chapter that looks out to the future of a movement, I have a conviction: *we must do our best to perpetuate this transformational work of God's Spirit in our local communities, to partner with him in the work of changing lives.* Yes, we bring every bit of innovation, ingenuity and synergy to the local mix. But if this movement is to sustain and bear maximum, lasting fruit, the best of what we bring must be continually submitted to the witness and the work of the Holy Spirit.

I have long been an active participant in the United States praying and planning for widespread spiritual awakening. But what I see most clearly are bright spots, "cities of refuge" rising and thriving on the landscape. God is sovereignly restoring the geographic identity and responsibility of the Body of Christ to partner together in winning and discipling the collective souls of their city. May more modern-day Antiochs arise to train and deploy leaders who can catalyze John 17 communities in other places. May Yahweh-Jireh, the Master Maker of all trends that truly transform, continue to keep his hand on these city gospel movements throughout the world, and bring forth much fruit.

Chapter Eight

Discerning and Dealing with High Level Spiritual Darkness in your City

Advancing God's kingdom in any measurable way puts us on holy ground. But it can also be hazardhous ground. If Nehemiah is our Old Testament prototype for city repair work, we should get the drift that enemies of God and his purposes are always lurking in the shadows. I'm introducing a topic that may seem complex, but can be initially understood with a simple hypothesis. If, in your community, you are seeing increased health in the Body of Christ, an increase of corporate prayer that is united and fervent, and an increase of collaboration that proclaims and demonstrates the gospel, then you can expect some "push back." I don't want to presume or predict this, but rather prepare you for it. Our highest aim is to see an increased number of people following Jesus. We would all readily concur that authentic "transformation" of people's lives is catalyzed by the power of the Holy Spirit. In short, we are engaged in a supernatural endeavor that has implications for the eternal destinies of souls. Indeed, we are engaged in an endeavor of grave and glorious importance.

Dealing with "spiritual warfare" issues may not fit your theological grid. Engaging the content of this chapter may stir some discomfort, even fear. But whether you like it or not, or whether this fits your world view, any cadre of leaders in a city or region that gets serious about stewarding John 17 covenantal communities will attract some measure of negative attention from the adversary. If we set our hearts and hands to advancing a visible, functional model of kingdom community, let's understand that the devil is all about promoting a counterfeit kingdom, the anti-type of what you and I are all about. Learning to discern and deal with spiritual resistance is a part of this turf. In these pages, I'm going to bring a perspective you won't often find in discussions of "city transformation."

In March, 2008, I found myself pacing a children's playground on site at a Prayer Summit I was leading in a large US city. I rang Terri up on my cell. Attendance had fallen short, my worship minstrel cancelled out, and the afternoon session was dragging. Self-doubt was creeping on the edges of my psyche. An old, familiar not-so-friendly feeling was in play: "This just isn't gonna go, Lord. Done all I can do. Over, move on." The immediacy and strength of Terri's response startled me. Her gift of exhortation in high gear, she gave it to me straight: "Get off that playground, get back into that room, and the Lord will show you what to do. This is *his* battle, not yours. *He* wants this city!"

I needed that word, and heeded it. As I began the walk back, a fresh word in my inbox: *"Contend for the city!"* In our meeting room, I pulled the "embers" back together, shared my heart: "Brothers, the devil hates what we're up to here. I believe we need to go to our knees, and *contend for the kingdom of God to increase in this city.*" We engaged, immediately and fervently. The oppression began to lift. After dinner, we moved into a meaningful, productive evening of worship and prayer. I retired that night with a hint of hope. The next morning, 8:32, our worship minstrel strolled in the door, keyboard in hand, "Sorry I didn't make it yesterday, but I'm ready to go." I am being honest here—within 10 minutes, the manifest presence of God was flooding the room, Baptists and Pentecostals, Anglos and African-Americans, boomers, busters and millenials soaking in the Father's favor. *To seriously contend for an increase of kingdom presence in a city, to seriously threaten the status quo, is to provoke a counter-contention from the hordes of hell.* Anyone who has been at this any length of time will tell you what I am saying here is neither hype nor paranoia, but resistance from a real foe who refuses to say "no" quickly or easily.

It is a mistake to be simplistic and reductionistic in our view of spiritual warfare. There is no "silver bullet" strategy through which we launch a "surface-to-air" missile that knocks out the devil's command post, and unleashes unity and revival. Dealing with darkness is an on-going component of a citywide mission. We're familiar with the high point of Jesus' priestly prayer, asking the Father to bring his disciples into organic oneness similar to the relational cohesion of the Godhead itself. But let's back up to the beginning of the prayer, verse 2: the Father granted Jesus "authority over all people that he might give eternal life to all those you have given him." Jesus possesses the highest authority in heaven and earth. And what is ultimately in his domain is the bestowal of eternal life. As deceiver, destroyer, and archenemy of the Christ, it is Satan's aim to distract, and, if possible, destroy this mission of redemption.

Jesus gets very specific: he asks for those who follow him to be brought into "complete unity" (17:23), for them to "have the full measure of my joy within them" (17:13). How profound is that? *The reality of the love and joy of Jesus flowing through his Body validates the authenticity of his Messiahship to an unbelieving world. Satan dreads the very prospect of this oneness being put on display.* Thus, an additional, explicit component of Jesus' intercession: "Holy Father, *protect* them by the power of your name—*so that* they may be one as we are one" (17:11). And again, "My prayer is not that you take them out of the world but that you *protect them from the evil one*" (17:15). Friends, in any community, we can only walk in the witness of covenantal oneness when we receive this vital benefit of Jesus' priestly intercession. In our everyday insurance lingo, this is an "umbrella" liability policy designed to cover exposure to risk.

As a practitioner and coach, here's my hypothesis. Wherever there is potential for authentic oneness among Jesus' followers, there also will be an insidious, unholy hatred that emanates from the counter-kingdom. To be honest, this resistance is not always overtly demonic, from the "outside." Often, the most sophisticated and damaging resistance comes from within the camp, where human ego, posturing, ambition or hurt feelings get in the way of God's purposes. Time and again, I have watched the Holy Spirit plant the seeds of the Psalm 133 commanded blessing into the soil of soft hearts. I have seen a remnant of men and women embrace Jesus' impartation of covenantal love, and open a door for an authentic John 17 witness of oneness. But then the growth and increase seems to go dormant, sometimes dry up altogether. When the "self stuff" of pride, posturing or control steps in, the favor of the Lord may seemingly retreat for a season. In one city overseas I labored in for several years, a key relationship "blew up" in one meeting, and momentum was lost. I just recently got word of a fresh group of young leaders rising up in that city, re-digging the wells, re-watering the seeds. *When the Lord is in our equation, nothing is ultimately lost. Seeds that have been planted through sacrifice, faith and obedience, remain in the soil of a city, ready for a fresh watering at a future time, in another season.* Kingdom life that might seem stifled by human stuff in a current season, might return in a future season through a fresh watering of the Word and the Spirit.

For those called to move God's kingdom forward in a specific community, let's face the facts. We must learn to discern subterfuge like this, put defensive covering in place and employ the skills of a spiritual warrior. Sure, King David was a "man after God's heart," with an unparalleled depth of devotional life, but he was also a man familiar with assaults from his enemies: "Contend, O Lord, with those who contend with me; fight against those who fight against me" (Ps. 35:1).

Intercessory Prayer Warfare: a Corrective Perspective

In the late 1960's, I was disillusioned by nominal "churchianity," and commenced a serious quest for truth. I was a classic "sixties religious seeker," meandering for three years into a multitude of metaphysical dead-ends. In his mercy, God the Father "gave me" to Jesus (John 17:2). I was set free from sophisticated, high-level deception. So, when I pondered a topic for my Masters thesis at Asbury Seminary in the fall of 1974, I sought out to research the biblical understanding of Paul's revelation of "principalities and powers." I discovered that these were high level angelic beings, the "Darth Vadars" of Satan's domain, whose role it was to deceive and draw to "the dark side" as much of humankind as they could, through any means.

By the time I connected with various prayer movements in North America in the late 1980's, the emphasis on high-level warfare was coming on the radar. There was keen interest identifying presumed principalities and powers of evil that ruled over cities and regions. Aggressive strategies were introduced and practiced. It was not uncommon to be in a meeting with prayer warriors raising arms and voices, adrenalin pumping, commanding certain ruling spirits to vacate the region. One respected theologian referred to this approach as a "spiritual technology," a quid-pro-quo mindset: "do *this* and you'll get result." In this context, I introduced in my first book, *The Believers Guide to Spiritual Warfare (1990),* a chapter in which I developed a "corrective perspective" on to how do deal with such high level spiritual resistance. In April, 2011, Regal re-released this book, with forty percent new material, and an upgraded chapter on this topic, Chapter 11, "Understanding and Practicing Intercessory Prayer Warfare." This chapter is my "magna carta" statement on the topic. I commend the book for its balanced, practical approach to "in-the-trenches" everyday warfare. But I particularly commend Chapter 11. Here's a summary quotation from that earlier work:

> "Here is my approach. In line with Jesus' word to His disciples (see Luke 10:17-20), our primary purpose is to proclaim the gospel, minister the power of the kingdom and trust the Holy Spirit for writing new names in the book of life. Power encounters must not be our preoccupation. We must not fall prey to the danger of embarking on a holy crusade to rid the world of evil. If our vision of God aching for the lost is blurred by a commando operation against the gates of hell, we miss the point." [1]

When we get serious advancing authentic kingdom community, resistance from the evil one is all too real. When it manifests we need to face it squarely and deal with it biblically.

Getting Perspective

I want to take this subject further and deeper, offering practical ways to engage spiritual warfare resistance in the community context. When describing satanic resistance, it is important to stay anchored in biblical revelation, and not wander into anecdotal storytelling. Paul warned the saints in Ephesus to guard against giving the devil a "foothold" through a failure to confess and resolve anger. In his second letter to the saints of Corinth, he shared that believers have an arsenal of weapons strong enough to "demolish strongholds" (2 Cor. 10:4), which he defines as "arguments and every pretension that sets itself up against the knowledge of God." This points to ideas, ideologies, philosophies, even behaviors and lifestyles that are contrary to God's truth. James employs a different imagery: don't allow bitterness, envy or selfish ambition to serve as a "harbor" (an opening) for demonic invasion. A stronghold may thus take root in a false philosophy, an alternative religion, or a pattern of repetitive, unresolved sin.

So, let me introduce a spiritual warfare "chicken and egg" question. Does idolatry or iniquity in a geographic place invite the activity of evil spirits, or is it the other way around? Do spirits of darkness work to entice human beings—non-Christians and Christians alike—into moral compromise? Which comes first? In nature, there are certain animals that contribute to one another's survival in a symbiotic relationship. Similarly, it seems, human sin is energized by evil spirits, and evil spirits gain increased power where there is heightened occurrence of sin. In another earthy illustration, we can say that rats are attracted to garbage. Remove the garbage, and the rats lose interest. Therefore, *the key to breaking spiritual strongholds in a city is not to go on a campaign to rid the heavens of spiritual pollutants, but rather for God's people to rid themselves of unholy habits that allow the enemy to perpetuate his grip on their lives.*

At some point of this journey, the power of God's kingdom has to trump the power of human culture. Recently I visited a major city in the Southeastern United States, casting vision for a Leaders Prayer Summit. In my sharing, I made reference to spiritual warfare influences in a city. Returning to that reference, one of the leaders spoke up, "It's no secret that this city has some kind of dark stronghold of mistrust, competition, and strife. You can see it in the early settling of this region with blood feuds among clans, like the notorious Hatfields and McCoys. Well, that spirit has in some way infected the Body of Christ here. Sometimes we seem to behave more like Hatfields than brothers in Christ." In another city, a couple hundred miles away, a leader shared, not so humorously: "Friend, this is the 'Bible belt,' and we're the buckle on the belt! People *love* their religion here, and are proud of it!" The city boasts a plethora of congregations, denominations and religious organizations.

Every city has its history, with distinct influences. Any people living in any place over time will open revolving doors to demonic influence. And the pathway that leads towards breakthrough—exposing and expelling the influences of darkness—is not deploying commando teams. The way forward is to grow God's kingdom in his way, in his time. Here's a simple re-cap of a progression I see from Ephesians that I share in *The Believers Guide to Spiritual Warfare*. Paul states matter-of-factly that saints in a city "do not wrestle with flesh and blood" (6:12). How are men and women of the kingdom to "wrestle" with the evil one? We embrace God's provision of authentic *unity*, rooted in *humility* (2:11-4:16). We walk in ethical *purity*, as individuals, and in community (4:17-5:21). Then, and only then, can the church in a city come into a place of *corporate authority*, to stand together exposing and overcoming our common enemy. *The progression is clear: living authentically in unity, humility, purity, fully accountable to one another, enables us to stand together in corporate authority.*

"A Model to All Believers"

So, where might we find this model explicitly in Scripture? What might a "model city" really look like? Paul goes out on a limb bragging on the saints in Thessalonica. Of any of the cities Paul visited and ministered to, these folks seem to "get it, and live it" incarnationally. "You became a model to all the believers in Macedonia and Achaia. The Lord's message rang out from you" (1 Thess. 1:7, 8). The Apostle commended them for their reputation for turning from idols to the living God. But without question, their greatest strength, the beacon light that shone forth from this city, was the authenticity of their affection. Paul pauses to pray, "May the Lord make your love increase and overflow for each other and for everyone else" (3:12). Here's a concrete, demonstrable answer to the most passionate part of Jesus' prayer to his Father (John 17).

Now, tracking with our current focus, here's an interesting observation. I don't think I'm reading between the lines, but rather discerning a level of negative spiritual activity. Paul said that he had been trying to come to Thessalonica, "again and again" to visit and encourage these believers, "but Satan stopped us" (2:18). Why would Satan work so hard to inhibit Paul's visit? We see in the text that he could hardly wait to inquire about the integrity of their faith: "I was afraid that in some way the tempter might have tempted you and our efforts might have been useless" (3:5). In view of the apostolic mantle on Paul, Satan did not want him stepping back into this model city. He dreaded the very thought of further apostolic impartation that would strengthen the beauty and testimony of this community even further.

And, in his closing remarks, he employs overt warfare language, "you are all sons of the light and sons of the day." He exhorts them to put in place the breastplate of faith and love, and the helmet of salvation. In short, *here's my premise: our archenemy is relentless in his efforts to undermine and destroy any authentic expression of a healthy Body of Jesus Christ.* As practitioners of city movements, we're foolish and ill equipped if we ignore this reality, and vulnerable if we fail to equip ourselves with God's provision of defensive armor and the offensive weapons.

Looking at his second epistle, it is no surprise that Paul warns the believers at Thessalonica about the deep deception that will come towards the close of the current age, and the rebellion that accompanies the work of the "man of lawlessness" (2 Thess. 2:3). They could handle this deeper revelation. Why? Because they had firsthand experience of satanic opposition. And here is the Apostle's confidence in God for this expression of a bona fide "city church" from New Testament times: "The Lord is faithful, and he will strengthen and protect you from the evil one" (2 Thess. 3:3). But it is also clear that this divine provision of protection is predicated upon Paul's exhortation to them to keep walking in obedience (3:4, 5). *The provision of divine protection is applied when we walk in faith. Essentially, this is similar to the petition Jesus asked of his Father for his followers: a divine covering, anchored in the virtue of the Lord's own name and character, but activated by the authenticity of affection and obedience.*

"Live as Children of Light"

In my perspective, the book of Ephesians is the pinnacle of Paul's theology of the Church. Ephesus was one of the cities that received the dual commendation and correction from Jesus (Rev 2:1-7). We understand from Acts 19 this place of strategic influence in Asia Minor was the throne of the goddess Artemis. It is no surprise therefore, that Paul explains "our struggle is not against flesh and blood…but against the spiritual forces of evil in the heavenly realms" (Eph. 6:12). The atmosphere of this city was charged with idolatrous, demonic presence! And yet, in a place where the devil contends for control, Paul unveils a deeper revelation of God's purpose:

> *"His intent was that now, through the church, the manifold wisdom of God should be made known to the rulers and authorities in the heavenly realms" (Eph. 3:10)*

The Body of Christ, bonded in organic, heart-to-heart unity, is to be a channel of light, a focused laser that beams the glory of God for all to see. I believe Paul is saying here, "Look at this amazing plan. God planned it and executed it. Now here, the redeemed, brought into one living Body, a household of faith, we get to declare to men and angels, that the grace of God made known in Jesus Christ *works!*"

The "wisdom" is God's plan, in place even before human history began, to provide a sacrifice for human sin. It is "manifold," multi-faceted, foretold and worked out over centuries through patriarchs, prophets, priests and kings. And here's the beauty of this verse. *This is not some ethereal, cosmic plan. Rather, it is revealed through real people, living in real communities, sharing a common grace, and declaring to earth and heaven alike, "God's wisdom works!"* The devil and his cohorts sow seeds of suspicion and mistrust, perpetuating the lie that a Jew is superior to a Gentile, a man superior to a woman, white skin better than black. But through the blood of Jesus, all prejudicial barriers are broken, and "one new man" now has "access to the Father by one spirit" (Eph 2:18). Brothers and sisters, in our own communities, it is our privilege to posture ourselves as the lens through which Redeemer-God beams the beauty of his plan to men below and angels above.

Here's the practical instruction. In view of this amazing revelation, Paul exhorts his fellow believers: "Be completely humble and gentle; be patient, bearing with one another in love. Make every effort to keep the unity of the Spirit through the bond of peace" (4:2, 3). *In the day-to-day reality of walking and working with fellow believers, this is work!* In the rest of chapter 4, he exposes the "dark side" of human attitudes and behaviors that play into the devil's hands: anger, bitterness, slander, malice. He makes a specific point about anger. If we justify our reactive resentment or anger against a brother or sister, and refuse to repent and resolve conflict, we run the risk of the enemy getting a "foothold," a place of influence. Does this danger relate only to anger? I think not.

If I justify anger, bitterness, judgment, or outright criticism of a brother or sister, with a heart hardened to the convicting work of the Spirit, I give the enemy an opening.

So, as we are walking and working together in our city, laboring to offer a secular culture a witness of oneness, we need to practice what Paul is preaching. It is a formidable challenge keeping relationships in right order, and doors closed to enemy influence. Across a city, it takes even greater diligence walking in integrity. This calls for gatekeeping leaders that discerningly watch for strained relationships. This requires a functional accountability. Paul is straight up with two "Don't's:" "Don't grieve the Holy Spirit…Don't give the devil a foothold." These warnings come clearly in the context of walking together in community.

And so Paul challenges the saints in Ephesus to "live as children of light" (5:8), exposing the lies and deeds of darkness, and displaying a radical dichotomy between the kingdoms of God and Satan. In the early to mid-1990's, many well-meaning city reachers mapped out presumed enemy strongholds and engaged in strong prayer warfare. But *here's the reality: nothing "outside" will move and go anywhere if things "inside" the Body of Christ are out of line!* We can shout and dance all we like, but if there is sin in the camp, the enemy will scoff at our best efforts and stay put. But when we strive to be "imitators of God" (5:1), honoring one another with pure hearts and resolving our conflicts, principalities have nothing to hang on to. Let's be honest. We're all imperfect people in process. We carry offenses and feelings towards one another, we drag our feet resolving our issues. If getting all of this right all the time depended on you and me, we would be "toast" most of the time! But the love of God covers a multitude of our sins and stumbles, and leads us to repentance and obedience.

Discerning and Dealing with Spiritual Attack

Earlier I shared that the holy ground of increased health of Christ's Body in a city may also become hazardous ground. From the beginning of my ministry call in 1972, I have worked hard at sharing a perspective on spiritual warfare that is "reasoned and seasoned." I don't want to give the enemy more credit than he deserves. In this arena, too many go off the tracks finding a demon lurking behind every problem, from migraine headaches to a prodigal child to financial shortfall.

So, a word of wisdom up front. Life itself is "uphillish." Whether you are a Christian or not, every one of us has to contend with our own propensities towards sin and self-centeredness. We have natural personalities that have upsides and downsides. We're all subject to "genetic roulette." Anything lurking in the genetic pool can "land" on anyone: cancer, Parkinsons, depression, diabetes, chemical dependence, psychiatric disorders, all kinds of problems common to humankind.

Sure, believers have access to the grace of God, his word, the Holy Spirit and prayer to find spiritual victory in their infirmities and adversities. We can also choose to walk in wisdom, improving nutrition, reducing stress, and taking medicines that alleviate symptoms. On top of genetics, many have grown up in dysfunctional, unhealthy families of origin, and suffer the wounds of emotional abuse, an alcoholic parent or a painful divorce. *Honestly, most of what I find in the lives of redeemed and unredeemed souls is an array of such vulnerabilities common to humankind.* At one level or another, most of us are in process of coping with physical infirmities, emotional pain, or both. Most of our "clay pots" are cracked in one way or another (anger, worry, anxiety, sexual temptation). But here's the good news. The believer has access to the love and grace of God, and can seek healing of painful wounds, and sealing of cracks of vulnerability.

So, life itself is a hard go. Some seem to have lives that are far more "uphillish" than others. Some seem to slide through or skate past trials and adversities, unscathed. But wherever you find yourself on the grid of "uphillishness," let me re-state my working premise: if you, your spouse or family gets serious about advancing God's kingdom, e.g., by stepping into a leadership role, praying for an unreached people group or going on a short-term mission, someone else steps up, scopes you out and tries to scare you off. The adversary may suddenly give you increased negative attention.

So, if you are engaged in a holy endeavor to advance a Jesus-led movement in your community, issues that you find to be normal and **"uphillish,"** *may begin to have an overlay of the* **"hellish."** The enemy may turn up the heat, looking to exploit vulnerabilities, work his way into a crack or trip you up in a besetting sin, getting a toehold, perhaps a foothold. This shift from normal to supra-normal should put a proper fear into the soul of anyone on the cutting-edge of city reaching.

Our adversary looks to mess with our minds, moods and moral weaknesses. As you read and reflect on what I'm sharing, pause for a moment, and inquire of the Lord. What are my chief vulnerabilities? What are the downsides of my personality? Is there a particular besetting sin that keeps tripping me up? Is there an emotional "thorn" that limits my ability to function in my calling? Here are a few examples:

- The darkness and debilitation of self-doubt, "I'm crazy…I'm inadequate…I'm over my head"
- Barrage of fear/terror: intimidation
- Heaviness/oppression: a blanket of darkness that does not lift
- Strain in a relationship that turns obsessive and oppressive
- A "thorn," e.g., melancholy, emotional damage, fear of man, excessive worry

It is not my purpose here to be comprehensive, but merely illustrative of what spiritual oppression might look and feel like. So, if you, your spouse, a good friend or colleague suspects an enemy assault, here are some helpful responses.

Breaking Through Personal Oppression: Practical Steps

First, be straight up honest and deal with any current issues of sin. Carefully walk through Ephesians 4:17 through Chapter 6, focusing on Paul's two "don't's: "Don't grieve the Spirit," and "Don't give the devil a foothold." Simply ask the Spirit to search your life and expose any compromises that make you vulnerable to the enemy's accusation and abuse.

Then let brother James work you over, soaking in James 4:1-10. Obey his counsel: "wash your hands you sinners, and purify your hearts, you double-minded." Get your heart right with the Lord, and then tell the devil to take a hike.

Second, if you are dealing with any "cracks" that make you vulnerable, resolve afresh to pursue a pathway that leads to a healing and sealing of those cracks. This could mean finding a counselor, or meeting with someone gifted in emotional healing prayer. Ask the Lord to guide you to a resource that will shed further light on your journey.

Third, seek the Lord, and ask your spouse and trusted friends to expose any downsides of your personality the enemy might try to exploit. I have to become fully responsible for my responses to people, to minimize offense. Years back a dear colleague, Jim Herrington, a founding member of the Mission Houston leadership team, shared this provocative thought: "I must be concerned about what I don't know that I don't know about myself." This speaks to "blind spots," aspects of my personality that may inadvertently offend others, or give the enemy an opening. Ruth Haley Barton, in *Strengthening the Soul of Your Leadership,* exhorts her readers to honestly explore the "unattended dark side" of their personal journeys and personalities. She quotes Gary McIntosh and Samuel Rima from their work *Overcoming the Dark Side of Leadership:* [2]

> "The dark side is actually a natural result of human development. It is the inner urges, compulsions,

and dysfunctions of our personality that often go unexamined or remain unknown to us until we experience an emotional explosion or some other significant problem that causes us to search for a reason why."

Ruth then goes on to say, "All of us have a shadow side to our leadership…the personal insecurities, feelings or inferiority, and need for parental approval (among other dysfunctions) that compel people to become successful leaders are often the very same issues that precipitate their failure." [3] So, when you find yourself engaged in citywide leadership at some level, and also find yourself "in the fray" of spiritual conflict, ask the Holy Spirit, ask your spouse, your closest co-workers, to bring these hitherto undiscovered dark corners of your soul into the light. I assure you, if you choose to ignore, deny and fail to deal with your dark side, the enemy will find a way to work it to his advantage. I'm sure the apostle Paul could unpack a ton here about the personal "thorn" he references in 2 Corinthians 12, or Peter his "sifting" experience.

If we're going to steer clear of being vulnerable to spiritual warfare we have to increasingly take seriously the blind spots and rough edges of our personalities. In our own regional movement in Oregon, Terri and I are committed to keeping "short accounts," quickly resolving relationships that go awry. On the positive side, we also carry a pro-active posture of covering fellow kingdom colleagues with prayer and blessing. I love how Oswald Chambers expresses this: "As a saved soul, the real business of your life is intercessory prayer. Whatever circumstances God may place you in, always pray immediately that His atonement may be recognized and is fully understood in the lives of others as it has been in yours" [4]

Fourth, we have to carry a high level commitment to "watch one another's backs." I encourage anyone seriously engaged leading a community or regional movement to be quick to send up a "prayer flare" (e-mail, phone call, text or twitter) when you suspect a spiritual assault. More and more, I find myself addressing city leaders with this question: "Is there anything happening in your mind, mood, relationships or family that feels like spiritual warfare? Is there any way I can intelligently pray for you with authority?" If advancing the kingdom collaboratively in your city is at the core of your calling, I believe it is imperative for you to put in place a small band called to the ministry of intercession. Start small, build a core, and communicate succinctly your assignments, prayer points and a few key Scriptures.

I have learned this practice the hard way, by taking some serious "hits," and belatedly asking for help. The movement in Skopje, Macedonia offers great hope to the whole Balkan region for reconciliation, healing and spread of the gospel. In October, 2011, in the middle of the annual Leaders Prayer Summit, a spiritual "torpedo" simultaneously hit both me and Sasha, the point man for Skopje. At 4:30 AM, I sent out a "prayer flare" to my inner core of trusted intercessors, and four hours later drew Sasha aside, praying in authority, asking God to lift the oppression.

Here's my point: we must be vigilant, being on watch for ourselves and our colleagues, our "band of brothers" in the trenches, ready to run to our Lord's provision given us in Psalm 91:

> *"If you make the Most High your dwelling—then no harm will befall you…for he will command his angels concerning you, to guard you in all your ways" (91:9-11).*

What a comforting promise! But the conditional caveat that releases this provision is in verse 15:""He will call upon me, and I will answer him. I will be with him in trouble."

Fifth, if you suspect or discern you, your family or ministry is under spiritual attack, step up, get some backbone, and "go to war!" God's weapons of warfare *work!* Ask the Lord, with your spouse and/or colleagues, to help you discern spiritual resistance, and then turn to him for help. Recognize also our human tendencies a) to consider everything *but* spiritual attack (being overly cognitive, ignorant or in denial), b) to press through an oppressive episode alone, and in our own strength, and c) to be tardy and tentative taking immediate authority in prayer. Even if your discernment is "mushy," and your trial has nothing to do with the devil, there is nothing to lose, and a lot to gain, calling on the Lord.

Simply employ the basic self-protective measures you learned in boot camp. Re-position your shield of faith, and pray immediately (pro-actively, pre-emptively). Remember, *there is no right formula for this prayer to be effective. You need not be oratorically correct. Just cry out to God from your heart, follow the stirrings of His Spirit, invite his help, and command any enemies of Jesus Christ to flee immediately.* Speak the Scriptures (sword of the Spirit, the "rema"), and pronounce any enemy schemes sent against you broken.

Here's a simple, succinct bottom line. Jesus acknowledged the reality of a real enemy who has power to loose real assaults against the servants of God: "the prince of the world is coming. He has no hold on me" (John 14:30). The warfare is real. It may get more subtle and sophisticated as our callings get more strategic. But we must learn to discern these assaults, turn more quickly to the Lord for help, and not allow anything of darkness to "land" on us, like a good defensive boxer veering away from his opponent, "you didn't lay a glove on me!"

Spiritual Warfare Issues in the Earliest "City Churches"

There is additional biblical data from Revelation 2 and 3 I would like to briefly add to this conversation. While there are vastly different approaches to interpreting this piece of literature, I am interested in the "dictation" of messages John took from the Lord given to believers resident in seven cities in Asia Minor. Some interpreters see these as 1) words to the actual historical places, 2) representative of seven future epochs of the development of the Church, or 3) both historical and allegorical, addressed to saints in real cities, but also meaningful for all readers. My interest is in looking at these seven venues as the earliest, identifiable expressions of the "city church," and to address the question, what were Jesus' central concerns for his followers?

Discerning and Dealing with High Level Spiritual Darkness in your City

In Revelation 2 and 3, there is a striking amount of reference to the work of the devil, and to classic spiritual warfare issues. Clearly, Jesus issues a contextual commendation to His Body in each venue that is specific and accurate to the historical situation. He is kind to practice a "plus, minus, minus, plus" approach, first pointing out positive things he sees in his followers, followed by some straight-up rebukes, and ending with a positive challenge to walk in obedience. *In each message, we see the pattern of commendation, correction and challenge.* As I have read and reflected on these letters numerous times, our Lord's bottom line concerns seem to boil down to compromise in three areas: immorality, idolatry and doctrinal deception. I'll not take time here to document these issues, but Jesus brings them up over and over. I believe he is saying, "Stay true to me, stay close to me. There is an enemy—a cunning and insidious serpent—working hard to lead you away from truth and into idolatry."

In his words to the saints that reside in Ephesus and Laodicea, Jesus seems most offended by their diminished affection for him. This is the heart of the issue. In his second letter to the believers in Corinth, Paul nailed it: "I am afraid that just as Eve was deceived by the serpent's cunning, your minds may somehow be led astray from your sincere and pure devotion to Christ" (2 Cor. 11:3). Jesus' main concerns were the closeness and constancy of relational intimacy with himself, and commitment to walking in the truth.

Here's where I'm going with this. In the real life laboratories of our own "city church" expressions, we would be wise to give heed to Jesus' words to these seven cities, and discern the snares of the serpent in our own culture. What would Jesus warn us about today? What forms of idolatry would he expose? As we engage growing the kingdom in our communities, let's keep a close eye on one another, let's keep accountable, and let's keep listening to any in our midst gifted with discerning of spirits.

And keep crying out for discernment in a season of spiritual danger, for yourself, your children and grandchildren, and for the Body of Christ in the city where you serve. May we truly hear the Lord Jesus clearly, today, in our own context, exposing the idolatries of our culture, and calling us to seek and abide only in him, empowered to overcome the age-old subtleties of the serpent.

Dealing with Systemic Spiritual Strongholds

In the early years working with city movements, I made attempts to structure and sequence initiatives aimed at exposing and weakening enemy strongholds. In my understanding, a "stronghold" is a belief, mindset or behavior that runs contrary to the word and will of God (2 Corinthians 10:3-5.) A stronghold may manifest at multiple levels, in the spiritual realm, in and through institutions (governmental, religious, economic, educational), and within individuals. For our purposes here, our question is this: *how can a united, praying Body of Christ in a city/region effectively identify, expose and weaken the influence of spiritual strongholds that negatively influence institutions and individuals?*

Let me offer first a word of wisdom. When dealing with a cunning adversary, we must guard against coming up with a plan of action, like a group of commandos executing a covert operation. Rather, we need to be well trained in the skills of discernment and prayer, and carefully follow the leading of the Holy Spirit. Our first priority is to be *pro-active* strengthening the health of the local Body, and not be prematurely *re-active* to what the enemy is up to.

1. Build a sustainable culture of prayer in your city.

In the early chapters of Acts we see believers meeting regularly for fellowship and prayer. They were often "together," getting their hearts right with one another and with the Lord. They seemed to posture themselves regularly to hear and fear God's instruction. I believe a city movement would be wise to implement some form of a "rhythm" of prayer, a regular pattern of seeking God together, receiving his corrections and getting his directions. In my home city, this is a rhythm of prayer we have sustained over many years:

- **"CitiPrayer,"** one hour of corporate prayer Thursday, 11 AM, mixed gender, multi-generational, theologically diverse (evangelical); open to pastors, associates, non-profit leaders, mature intercessors, marketplace leaders. Predominant focus: interceding for our city (1 Tim. 2:1-5).

- **Emphasis on fasting and prayer,** January, each congregation/organization selects a week and structures its own approach, with prayer offered for needs in the church or ministry, the city, and the unreached.

- **"Adoration:"** last Sunday night of January, a citywide gathering for corporate worship and intercession.

- **Leaders Prayer Summit:** first week of February, Cannon Beach, OR, parallel Summits for men and women, with joint worship and intercession Tuesday night.

Whatever a pattern of prayer may look like, it is vital to provide a regular context for both leaders and churchgoers to be in God's presence. This is a clear practice that kept the book of Acts congregations alive to the Word of God, alert to the work of the enemy, and accountable to one another. *If we are truly serious about seeing the spiritual atmosphere in our community change, we must be committed long term to irrigating and saturating every sphere of social activity with the incense of united, fervent intercession.* And to put such a rhythm in place, it takes persevering leaders committed to keep prayer times on track, creative and meaningful for participants. Building a "culture of prayer" takes high intentionality, time and perseverance. Those guiding your movement must discern your own preferred rhythm, set it in place, and steward it well.

2. Resolve sin issues and broken relationships.

In every city I've worked in, there are always rifts between individuals, sometimes institutions—misunderstandings, offenses, disagreements—that need repair. In Chapter 6 I talked about these things as hindrances to collaboration. Paul makes a point that should unsettle us: unresolved anger (and by implication in context also resentment, malice, slander) opens a door to enemy influence (Eph. 4:27). The word "place" here is "topos," a geographic place of strategic advantage or influence. If we hope to gain ground exposing and expelling enemy influence from our cities, we need to be vigilant and diligent reconciling strained relationships.

In one city, a local pastor had effectively served on the citywide leadership team. He came into conflict with the elders of his congregation, and was dismissed with great pain and duress. The church asked him to not start another church in the city. He signed a statement to that affect. He then broke that promise, starting another congregation, drawing a core group of loyalists out of the original church. So, obviously, these hurts created strained relationships within the congregation, *intra-church issues.* But because of this man's role in the citywide expression of the Body, there also developed *inter-church issues,* with other pastors on the citywide team offended by this brother's lack of integrity and the sowing of seeds of division in the community.

Resolving these issues ended up taking years, not months. The devil was given an opening, and he took it. This agonizing process drained much of the joy from the citywide endeavor for a season, and distracted the focus of the leaders. *Here's the bottom line: whether there is a formal team of citywide leaders in place, or the city eldership is more informal and ad hoc, there must be a local spiritual community that is authentically accountable to one another.* The "one church, comprised of many congregations" must be diligent to obey the Word of the Lord, take initiative to resolve strained and broken relationships, and close doors to the devil's influence. The situation with Ananias and Sapphira in Acts 5 is the clearest New Testament illustration of this.

3. Mobilize your citywide intercessors.

In the early 1990's, I was strong on putting formal teams of intercessors in place. I spent a ton of time and energy working with pastors and intercessors in sincere attempts to identify and organize mature prayer leaders. I have since come to understand that the role of an "intercessor" is neither an office of the Church, nor a clear gift of the Spirit. *Every mature, fruit-bearing believer is called to be a man or woman of prayer.* I am convinced that one of the responsibilities of a disciple of Jesus is to be available to the promptings of the Spirit to intercede for fellow saints, unbelievers, and situations where God calls us to partner with his purposes. That said, I also believe God *does* call certain men and women to engage in a *ministry* of regular intercession. I have also often referred to these as "prayer warriors," folks that love to listen to the Lord, receive assignments and spend regular, extended time in prayer.

I have also discovered that when citywide intercession teams are established, it is a challenge sustaining them. Here are a few of the challenges: a) finding a mature leader who has both the proven character and skill sets to lead a team, b) finding a context or platform in which intercessors can communicate with pastors and other leaders what they are hearing and receiving, and c) dealing with tension that arises from the difference in "DNA wiring" between pastors and intercessors. Of necessity, pastors have to *engage the world as it is, and are thus realistic and pragmatic. Intercessors love to pray into the world that could be or should be,* and thus are more prophetic. So, whether a citywide prayer team is formal or more fluid, this tension will be present. And it can either create conflict, or an opportunity to creatively align these two callings alongside one another to release mutual appreciation and blessing. Personally, I am most appreciative of intercessors interceding for pastors and their families walking through a trial, or a congregation navigating a stressful season of transition.

Since the development of "houses of prayer" introduced by Mike Bickle at "IHOP" (International House of Prayer, Kansas City) and also by Pete Grieg in England (*Red Moon Rising,* the "Boiler Room" movement), there has been a proliferation of houses of prayer worldwide. We often hear the catchword "24/7" associated with this, reflecting the Kansas City model (fourteen years of round-the-clock worship and intercessory prayer and continuing). While this is a remarkable achievement, Mike and his staff are very clear that this was a specific and clear call from the Lord. They strongly caution others stirred to birth "24/7" prayer in a city or region to not set the bar of expectation too high. For example, it is a wonderful thing to simply provide a venue, leadership and worship minstrels for four to six to ten hours on a regular, weekly basis. Just pulling *this* off brings a huge increase of focused, intentional intercession in a city environment! We need simply to be open in any given city to how the Lord wants to implement the context/platform in which the leaders of congregations and organizations can interface with prayer warriors called to labor on the wall of the city (Is. 62:1-6).

4. "Exegete" your city.

This concept of "exegeting your city" is brilliant! This is a theological term that describes the endeavor of discovering and drawing out the originally intended meaning of a biblical text. As applied to a city, I first heard this discipline described by Dr. Ray Bakke at the 2008 National City Impact Roundtable in Boston. Simply put, this is an unpacking of the various components that contribute to the way things currently are in a community. Solomon exhorts time and again in his Proverbs to "cry out for understanding." Well, to exegete a city movement, for example, is to to discern why there might be high occurrence of gang violence, racial tension or poverty in a certain neighborhood. Our tendency is to throw a lot of influence or money at problem communities, instead of taking the time to uncover roots of pain or injustice that drive the surface symptoms.

Bakke encourages conversations with people on the ground and "in the know," asking such questions as: "Why is this neighborhood like it is today? Who holds and exercises power? Who is marginalized, and why?" Once you begin tracing from fruits back to roots, the hard data enables prayer warriors to intercede with informed intelligence, and enables practitioners to design action plans to repair broken walls and burned gates in the community. (See Appendix, "Reading Your City," by Glenn Smith).

Initiatives that Weaken Strongholds

Let me re-iterate a few of the concrete steps that leaders of a community gospel movement can initiate that serve to expose and weaken systemic spiritual strongholds in a region.

- **Taking a cue from both Acts and the Pauline Epistles, put a corporate prayer rhythm in place** that works best in your context. As faithful saints persevere to offer the Lord the incense of their supplications, I believe he is faithful to cover our communities with his shalom and spiritual protection.

- **Produce a time line of your city's journey,** with two historical tracks: 1) spiritual high water marks, events, seasons of favor and spiritual breakthrough, individuals/institutions that have sown into your community. "Stand on the shoulders of men and women of faith who have preceded your endeavors. And 2) list things from the "dark side" of your corporate journey, idolatry, immorality occurrences of injustice. Expose the roots of current societal pain, and ask the Holy Spirit to guide you as to when and how your kingdom community can repent of and diminish the power of systemic, subterranean sin strongholds. Look to Ezra 9, Nehemiah 9 and Daniel 9 for guidance.

- **Care for the poor and the marginalized.** There is an unmistakable "If-Then" condition from the Lord in Isaiah 58: here's the kind of "fast" (sacrifice) that pleases the Lord: "to loose the chains of injustice and untie the cords of the yoke, to set the oppressed free and break every yoke" (58:6). "Then," says the Lord, I will bless you, I will answer when you call, I will be your rear guard, your light will rise in the darkness." *Without question, a key component for spiritual breakthrough in a city is to take this admonition seriously, and engage ministry to the poor and needy.* This may translate into food, linen and toiletry pantries, affordable housing, mentoring of troubled kids, job skills training, helping single moms.

- **Prayerwalk your neighborhoods.** Take God's favor and blessing to the streets, praying "on site with insight," lifting residents, schools, businesses, playgrounds, parks, government workers to the Lord's throne. In your own neighborhood, practice a "prayer, care, share" lifestyle witness, approaching neighbors with friendly conversation and/or acts of kindness. Be available for the release of the Lord's shalom into your city. You carry within you the greatest story ever told. Watch for open doors from the Holy Spirit to pray your way into a neighbor's story and heart. (See Appendix, "Short Form: Instruction for Prayerwalking")

- **Call the "city church" to citywide worship.** In my community saints have gathered the last Sunday night of January for the past five years for "Adoration," an evening devoted to worship and intercession. In Kingston, Ontario, believers gather citywide late May for "Kingdom Come," to celebrate their oneness in Jesus, and ask God's continued favor on "the King's Town." While leaders have more opportunity to build this kind of John

17 relationship, the "people in the pew" don't. When saints across a community gather to honor the Lord corporately, he honors us. I have come away from many such gatherings perceiving a "shift in the heavenlies," a positive change in the spiritual atmosphere, a change that only God can produce.

- **Watch for the Father's "fingerprints."** This may be the most important application I could share. To reiterate Solomon's wisdom, "Unless the Lord builds the house, we labor in vain. Unless the Lord watches over the city, we watch in vain" (Ps 127:1). In our city movements, we're often on the hunt for "what works," keen to pick up the latest, proven best practices, take them back to our city and do "plug and play." This can be flesh, even folly. The wisest thing we can do is to faithfully participate in our local prayer rhythm, pray without ceasing "Thy kingdom come, Thy will be done," and watch for where and what the Lord touches.

- **Engage in strategic, targeted intercession, in season, at the Holy Spirit's instruction.** If the Lord exposes and identifies any particular stronghold issues in your community, watch for opportunities opened by the Spirit to pray in authority to break them. I give the account in *The Believers Guide to Spiritual Warfare* a most amazing prayer gathering I participated in back in the early 1980's in Oregon. The leader of an international Hindu cult, Bagwhan Rajneesh, moved into Central Oregon with 5,000 fanatical devotees, stirring up all kinds of trouble, legal, political and spiritual. I was called to engage with other prayer warriors for three days of fasting and praying. One evening, right around 10 PM, our leader put up a holy shout, "It's done, we've broken through!" Our intercession turned from prevailing to celebrating. Within weeks, the cult unraveled from internal dissension, and within three months, the Bagwhan was deported, wandered from country to country for several more years, and died in India, with no followers, and no money. And here's the "rest of the story!" Young Life purchased the property, and converted it into "Wild Horse Canyon" youth camp, redeeming the land and touching the lives of young people for the gospel.

The Secret of Breaking Strongholds

In closing, let me try to make a complicated, controversial topic simple. *As you grow a city gospel movement, don't get overly obsessive or paranoid about what the enemy is up to.* This can become its own diversion. Keep your eyes and heart fixed on Jesus, and what he is doing in your community. Follow the clear progression I referenced earlier in Ephesians. Yes, Paul is spot on that we wrestle with high-level powers of darkness. But step back and begin with Paul's exhortation to walk in humility, embrace unity with brothers and sisters, and walk in ethical purity and accountability. On this foundation of holy obedience, when faced with enemy attacks, we stand together in corporate authority, and press through into victory. This gets sloppy. It's hard work, and we take enemy hits. Thus, give priority attention to vulnerabilities internal within the Body before you go ballistic battling forces external.

Watch for shifts, tipping points, grace gifts from the Lord. I often talk about things "shifting in the heavenlies," momentum, a gaining of spiritual ground. This is the Lord's prerogative. It may come in corporate worship, a grace anointing on a particular agreement in prayer, the reconciliation of a strained or broken relationship, or God's favor on a citywide event or project. When you discern something moving in the heavens, just thank God, celebrate the momentum, claim and hold the new ground. This is what brings change in the spiritual atmosphere over a city or region.

It is Yahweh's sovereign authority alone that subdues principalities and powers. Thus, I like, and often employ, the pattern David gives us for warfare in Psalm 35:1: *"Contend, O Lord, with those who contend with me; fight against those who fight against me."* That's it, in a nutshell. Better yet is Psalm 144:6, 7:

> *"Send forth lightning and scatter the enemies, shoot your arrows and rout them. Reach down your hand from on high; deliver me and rescue me from the mighty waters, from the hands of foreigners."*

When "up against it," I appeal directly and decisively to the sovereign authority resident in his name, and ask him to move swiftly to clear out any spiritual air pollution in my world, and, as guided, in my city. Depending on the nature and strength of the battle, relief is sometimes immediate, sometimes prolonged. Remember, this is real battle, and not a video game with an off button!

This, and this alone, is how strongholds of culture, demons and human flesh are broken. We're fooling ourselves if we think otherwise. As I close this chapter, I'm asking God to keep using my foolishness, and oftimes fickle, flagging faith to manifest his amazing strength. As you engage spiritual resistance in your city, remember that "the weapons we fight with are not weapons of the world. On the contrary, they have divine power to demolish strongholds" (2 Cor. 10:4).

Epilogue

Looking for the City That is yet to Come... but Already Here

"For we do not have here an enduring city, but we are looking for the city that is yet to come"
Hebrews 13:14

I began in Chapter 1 offering a theological perspective for citywide movements, the desire of our triune God for relationship, and a design to dwell among his people. One of the contexts for such "dwelling" has been the focus of this book, the "one church, comprised of many congregations" that finds expression in specific communities. My more activist readers will likely take issue with this approach, thinking it far too "churchy." But if I understand Acts, the Epistles and Revelation correctly, if we do our best to get relationships right (vertical with the Lord and horizontal with one another) walk in humility and holiness, all the while saturating our endeavors with prayer, *holy God is already in the equation, and will empower our endeavors.* My revivalist, "presence-based" friends will think me far too consumed with structures and plans. "Your approach involves too much human effort, and takes too long. If we get our hearts right, and get desperate enough, the Lord will 'show up!'" I pray for and expect his presence continually. But my overall experience over many years tells me that in any given community, members of Christ's Body still have so little revelation, and so much "stuff" (ego and ambition, theological pride, competition), it takes a "long obedience in the same direction" to see breakthrough and traction towards lasting transformation.

But the Lord sometimes gives a special and surprising grace. The saints in Siliguri, India experienced dramatic, measurable breakthrough and traction less than three years following their intentional embrace of Psalm 133 unity, and faithfully praying for their city every Saturday morning. In Abilene, West Texas, breakthrough and a change in the spiritual atmosphere of the city was palpable within a matter of months after their commitment to build John 17 unity across the city. In short, when we let God's Spirit break our hearts and align our prayers with his purposes, kingdom influence in any given community can accelerate dramatically. *There will always be a variety of approaches and applications.* How leaders choose to organize will differ. As I've shared throughout this book, there will be different vehicles, but if we're going to see lasting fruit that brings glory to God, he needs to be the fuel.

As I wrap up my thoughts, I would like to place the city gospel movement in a broader eschatological context. What are some of the wider implications of this work of the Holy Spirit in our time? Where might these expressions of John 17 covenantal kingdom community be going? How might the Lord want to use city movements to more effectively bring the gospel to the yet unengaged and unreached peoples still bound in the deceptive grip of false religions and secular lifestyles? Again, the bottom line objective of Jesus' prayer: "…so that the world will believe."

Many Christians I meet dream of being a part of a genuine moving of God's Spirit. I came into the kingdom in 1969, swept in on the wave of the "Jesus movement," a work of the Spirit that apprehended thousands of confused seekers like myself. I believe we are living now in the midst of a sovereign work of the Holy Spirit around the world focused on the end-time harvest. I began this book highlighting Yahweh's question through Isaiah, *"Where is the house you will build for me?" (Is. 66:2)*. I am convinced that God is bringing forth concrete answers to the deepest heart cry of his Son. I am encouraged by daily reports of city church expressions springing up worldwide, a healthy Body of Jesus Christ serving in the complex cultural, economic and political systems of humankind, allowing the life-giving presence of the Spirit to permeate the darkest corners and most difficult challenges of our communities. *"It's happening!"*

"Prototypical Foreshadowing:" A Touch of Heaven in the Here-And-Now

The author of Hebrews gets it right, we do not have on this earth an "enduring city." We are all pilgrims passing through, sojourners searching for a better place. Our world will remain marked and marred by sin, selfishness and satanic activity, until Jesus returns to reverse the curse of the Fall and redeem the creation. But do we not carry within us the vision seeds of a "city that is yet to come?" For thirty-five years, Black Butte Ranch in the Oregon Cascades has been Terri's and my favorite place for rest, rejuvenation and inspiration. Their promotional tag line, "There is a place." Well, friends, "there is a place" our Lord has prepared for all of us!

When most Christians think of a "holy city," their minds think Jerusalem. There is, of course, biblical precedent for Jerusalem being a model of kingdom life. This piece of real estate is of special interest to the Lord. Indeed, he is quite explicit about his ultimate design and desire for this city:

> "I have posted watchmen on your walls, O Jerusalem; they will never be silent day or night. You who call on the Lord, give yourselves no rest, and give him no rest till he establishes Jerusalem and makes her the praise of the earth" (Is. 62:6, 7).

As a veteran boots-on-the-ground practitioner, I have to ask, "What does this really mean? What are the implications of this revelation and call to prayer, for the word and will of God to be fully accomplished in a particular place, namely, Jerusalem?" At the conclusion of Isaiah 62, we have another window into God's heart longing for both his people, and this city: "They will be called the Holy People, the Redeemed of the Lord; and you (Jerusalem) will be called Sought After, the City No Longer Deserted" (62:12). Yes, this is a promise for a bright future for a particular city. But I believe this promise has implications in the here-and-now for New Testament believers, wherever they may dwell.

Epilogue

In a season of prayer during the third Men Meeting with God retreat with Jerusalem leaders in the year 2000, the Lord shared with me that we were experiencing a "prototypical foreshadowing" of his promises. I'm a word-crafter. I love new language. But I found myself asking, what does *that* mean? Surely, like portions of other prophetic writings, the Lord is pointing ahead to a future that is yet hoped-for. Yawheh gives us explicit, awe-inspiring descriptions in Isaiah 65:17-25 of what life under his reign will look like in this city: no more weeping, no more infant mortality, extended life and vitality, economic productivity, no misfortune, and the classic illustration, "the wolf and the lamb will feed together." What a hope…"there is a place!" But then I find it fascinating in the very next chapter, Yahweh poses the question: *"Where is the house you will build for me? Where will my resting place be?"* The immediate answer: with broken, humble people who welcome his presence.

It is neither biblical nor realistic to set our hopes on societal utopias. A perfect city or society will just not happen prior to Jesus' personal return. *So let's be honest and realistic about what we're really after: a healthy Body of Jesus Christ, in geographic locales, honoring and preferring one another in love, praying and obeying together, sowing the seed of the gospel among the lost, serving the least, and believing God to supernaturally increase the impact of his kingdom in every sphere of societal activity.* I believe any cadre of Christ-followers, in any place, may offer their hearts, in humble contrition, for the Lord's extended habitation. And I believe those saints may pray intentionally and fervently for a sustained influence of the kingdom—by the supernatural working of the Word and the Spirit—to impact and change the people in their daily lives.

So, *what do I really mean by "prototypical foreshadowing?"* I believe Paul sheds light on this by sharing a contrast between the earthly and heavenly expressions of "Jerusalem." In Galatians 4:24-26, he says that Hagar represents Mt. Sinai, the site where the law was given, and "the present city of Jerusalem, because she is in slavery with her children." The law carries with it the connotation of bondage. But Sarah, the mother of the promised seed, wife of Abraham, the father of faith, represents the heavenly, spiritual Jerusalem. Paul makes what first seems to be an odd, enigmatic statement: "The Jerusalem that is above is free, and she is our mother" (4:26). Clearly, Paul is illustrating the radical contrast of the Old and New Covenants. In figurative terms, he is describing the spiritual identity and heritage of New Covenant believers. For the Christian, the spiritual Jerusalem is the source of our life and nurture. As 21st century saints, we need to comprehend that our "citizenship is in heaven" (1 Pe. 3:20). Thus, if the heavenly Jerusalem, the model city that depicts freedom, is our "mother," this has profound implications for city-reaching practitioners.

The writer of Hebrews (I believe it is Paul) gives us further light. Contrasting again Sinai (law and bondage) and Zion (grace and freedom), he states, "you have come to Mount Zion, to the heavenly Jerusalem, the city of the living God" (He. 11:22). The language is explicit and concrete: *You "have come"* (already accomplished) to myriads of angels, to redeemed members of the church, to God himself, and "to Jesus the mediator of a new covenant." *The church—the company of the redeemed-- is now the locus and the focus of the heavenly Jerusalem. Collectively, believers--past, present future—the full host of God's angels, and the triune God comprise a heavenly society.* In Matthew Henry's terminology, the church is the "emblem of heaven." Note again the language: "You have come." Believers, walking together in faith, joined by the love of Jesus, are already active inhabitants, citizens of the "heavenly city," Jerusalem. Therefore, *we may regard ourselves as already being occupants of the holy city, and we are to live and act as if we are already partaking of its joys and blessings.*

Thus, the Body of Christ, serving as the locus of Mt. Zion, is not merely an inspired figure of speech. Rather, these are everyday saints taking Jesus' John 17 prayer seriously, and offering the Father, Son and Spirit a tangible place to dwell, an incarnational revelation of the Godhead, visible and accessible through real people, "so that the world will believe." Such sustained habitation, in the hearts of Christ followers, is a rare treasure, highly attractive, a compelling verification of Jesus' Lordship to the skeptical and secular culture that surrounds us.

Prophetic Perspective

Many would readily agree that we are likely in the final stages of history as we know it. I reference Jesus' words: "This gospel of the kingdom will be preached in the whole world as a testimony to all nations (ethne, people groups), and then the end will come" (Mt. 24:14). Well, I have in my hands a listing of the roughly twenty-eight hundred remaining language groups that are either yet "unengaged" or not yet fully "reached." Partnerships in the Body of Christ worldwide are being put in place to engage and reach these groups. I believe that John 17 communities are a part of God's plan to bring the light of the gospel to the remaining dark corners of our world. I believe the Lord of the harvest is now raising up modern day Antiochs, cities of refuge, **from which** trained kingdom ambassadors will go out to other cities, nations and people groups, and **to which** people will come for inspiration, training and impartation. I am convinced the Holy Spirit is preparing city movements around the world to participate in the completion of Jesus' Great Commission.

In March 2013, at an international gathering of kingdom leaders hosted at the International House of Prayer in Kansas City (IHOP), I witnessed an emerging partnership that quickened my faith afresh. Four of the participants (four among many) were YWAM, Cru (formerly Campus Crusade), IHOP and the Seed Company, an off-shoot of Wycliffe, joining forces and resources to target remaining unengaged and unreached people groups. Now, let's get this--this is a mix of charismatics and Pentecostals partnering with conservative evangelicals, tracking with a shared passion and collaborating on a common mission. What a fantastic development! Major mission organizations laying aside their differing theologies and methodologies and partnering to more effectively accomplish Jesus' two highest priorities.

That's just one piece. Here's another that has come onto my radar. In June, 2013 I was invited by Dr. Mac Pier, Senior Lausanne Associate for Cities, to participate in the Global Leadership Forum in Bangalore, India, sponsored by The Lausanne Movement ("The whole church taking the whole gospel to the whole world"). The main aim: to further catalyze increased collaboration towards the completion of the Great Commission. The Holy Spirit led us to launch the Global Urban Leadership Learning Community (GULCC), a first-ever international association of urban practitioners and theologians engaged in city movements in their nation or region. This is a timely development: connecting mature city movements in the West with emerging city movements in Asia, Africa, Latin America, Russia and the Middle East, forming relational and functional partnerships that focus on remaining unengaged and unreached peoples. In short, incarnational expressions of kingdom community that are relationally based, empowered by the Spirit and committed to a shared responsibility to witness to, win and disciple yet unreached peoples. Here's the strategy: engaging these "nations" (ethne) as the diaspora on our doorstep, folks from every tribe, tongue and culture living in our cities, with a John 17 witness of oneness.

Speaking of Jerusalem

I began my Prologue with a story taken from the first Leaders Prayer Summit I helped facilitate in North Israel in November, 1995. As an Epilogue, I'd like to close with another story. I believe Father God has yet unfinished family business with his Old Covenant people, the Jews, and Jerusalem, the city he chose for their habitation. We've spoken already of the role of John 17 communities in cities collaborating to bring the gospel to the remaining unengaged and unreached peoples in our world. Well, if we take Paul's word seriously, the gospel is "the power of God for the salvation of everyone who believes: first for the Jew, then for the Gentile" (Rom 1:16). Paul takes this on as a personal burden: "Brothers, my heart's desire and prayer to

God for the Israelites is that they may be saved" (Rom 10:1). We know gospel witness will come through individuals, in the context of relationship. That's a given. But what could be more attractive to spiritually minded Jews than putting on display healthy "one new man" expressions, vibrant John 17 communities, that which God originally wanted Israel to have, a "place to dwell" among his people?

As I conclude this work, I'd like to share a personal story, another piece of the "vision puzzle" I believe God is putting into place. From 1995 through 2001, I had the privilege of planting a model of Psalm 133 unity and John 17 community among a mix of Messianic and Gentile kingdom leaders in Israel, first in the Galilee Region, then Jerusalem, which led to a monthly gathering known as "Men Meeting with God." Over time, the brothers involved took further steps walking in oneness of heart. This ultimately led to a national model, "Sitting at Yeshua's Feet," an annual three-day gathering of kingdom-minded leaders of the Body of Christ from all over Israel. This gathering has now embraced some key Arab Christian leaders, fulfilling even further the Pauline vision for "one new man" in Jesus Christ (Eph. 2). Frankly, this is a remarkable story, a miracle of God's grace known to so few.

In September, 2010, I was invited to be a guest at the annual Sitting at Yeshua's Feet gathering. Praying and worshiping with four generations of Messianic leaders, singing in Hebrew, Arabic, Russian and English, was a personal high point, a foretaste of heaven, seeing an authentic John 17 multi-generational community of assorted Jewish and Gentile believers worshiping and walking together.

Epilogue

The day after this gathering, I was to depart Tel Aviv for my first visit to Beijing to have conversations with leaders of the house church movement about the possibility of birthing Prayer Summits in China. It was Friday afternoon. Sunset, the official commencement of Shabbat, was two hours off. I was to have dinner with my host and his family. Around 3 PM, the Holy Spirit stirred me. I was aware there were Houses of Prayer at the four compass points outside the gates of the Old City. I had previously prayed at two of them, the basement of the Mt. Zion Hotel to the West, the other on the Mt. of Olives. But I had been told about a house of prayer in the historic City of David, adjacent to the South Wall, a few hundred yards from the Dung Gate. I'd been given the names and number for a John and Una. At the City of David visitors center, I rang up Una. She guided me in through a predominantly Muslim neighborhood. We shared a brief introduction and a few pleasantries. I told her I was leaving for China the next morning. I walked around the prayer room, soaking it in. Then, surprisingly, Una spoke up, "Wait here, I have something I think you'd be interested in." She returned with a walking stick, and held it up for me to see Chinese characters carved in the handle, names of specific cities in China. "These were the first to come, last May, from cities in China. They stayed about a week, then disappeared. They left this walking stick. Is this of interest to you in any way?"

So, the man I was to meet the next day, on my very first visit to Beijing, happens to be the logistical coordinator for some sixty cities on the historic silk road trade route that extended from China, through the Middle East, back to Jerusalem.

Since the 1920's, house church leaders have received revelation, what they believe to be an assignment from the Lord, to witness their way back through the nations of the Middle East (mostly all Muslim), and ultimately bring a witness of the gospel to the Jewish people. Jesus gave his disciples the commission to witness starting in Jerusalem, "ground zero," extending ultimately to the "ends of the earth." Well, the believers in China believe they qualify as "the ends of the earth," some of the last to receive the gospel, and feel *they* are now "ground zero" for initiating a movement that will take the gospel back to the Jewish people. So, simply, the Lord has put on my heart a growing burden to pray into the emergence of Psalm 133 and John 17 communities in the cities and Provinces of China, bringing together leaders of the church that serve above ground ("registered church") and below ground ("house church").

As I've listened, actual plans are in process among Chinese believers, welcomed by indigenous believers to settle in specific cities, learning the local language, getting jobs, having families, trusting the Holy Spirit to open doors for witness. *Friends, might it be on God's heart to plant and prosper John 17 "one new man" communities in the many cities that lie between China and Jerusalem: Islamabad, Karachi, Kabul, Tehran, Dubai, Bhagdad?* I believe it is. I know this all sounds rather "out there." But I believe this is one aspect of how God is going to use city gospel movements to bring the light of the gospel to all peoples.

Epilogue

A High Calling: Catalyzing and Stewarding Kingdom Communities

Friends, as both theologian and veteran practitioner, this is a piece of the "macro-vision" I carry. But as we close, more importantly, let me also bring back into focus the "micro-vision." The content of this book has focused on the outworking of one of Jesus' deepest longings, to see his followers walking and working together in love and bearing fruit that will glorify the Father. In closing, I return to Yahweh's fatherly query, *"Where is the house you will build for me? Where will my resting place be?" (Is. 66:1)*. Regardless of what "macro visions" happen or don't happen, this can and should happen where you are planted, in your own neighborhood, where the Lord has called you to dwell. You can be a catalyst or participant building the "house of the Lord." You can set up a portable tent of meeting in your own "backyard." You can call others around you to an Ephesians 2:22 vision to assemble as "living stones," submitting to Jesus' Lordship, "being built together to become a dwelling in which God lives by his Spirit."

I pray this revelation stirs and settles into your own heart, and compels you to see an authentic kingdom expression increase in your community. Yahweh Shammah, the God who chooses to dwell with particular people in specific places, is answering the priestly prayer of his Son, the Lord of the harvest. "One, so that the world" will wake up and see the beauty of the Bride of Christ, believe, and receive the gift of life. Why not *you*? Why not *your* community?

About the Author

Founder and President of Frontline Ministries, Tom White conducts an international ministry catalyzing and developing citywide gospel movements, and teaching on the topics of spiritual formation, unity in the Body of Christ and spiritual warfare. Tom has emerged as a recognized innovator and practitioner in city transformation—building collaborative partnerships among kingdom leaders to more effectively reach their communities. He holds degrees from San Diego State University (B.A. Sociology, Minor in Religious Studies), and Asbury Theological Seminary (M.A. Theology).

Tom currently serves on the Leadership Cabinet of "Movement Day," an annual gathering of city movement practitioners hosted in New York City. He also designed and facilitates "City Advance," a leadership learning community for citywide leadership teams.

Tom and his wife Terri live in Corvallis, Oregon, giving leadership to the "Church of the Valley," a two-decade old movement of John 17 unity, prayer and kingdom collaboration in Oregon's mid-Willamette Valley.

Resources

Frontline Ministries

Additional copies of *The Practitioner's Guide* may be ordered through Good Place Publishing (www.goodplacepublishing.com), or by contacting the author. *The Believers Guide to Spiritual Warfare* may be purchased at discount from the author through email, text, voicemail, the Frontline blog site or Amazon.

Contact Information:

tntwhite07@gmail.com

www.flministries.org

541-760-0126

Ministry Offerings:

Tom is available upon request for the following:

Leadership Encounter:
   Connecting meaningfully with God and kingdom colleagues.
   - Residential retreats, 24-48 hour options

Ignite!
   Casting vision for a city gospel movement

   - Multi-sector mix of pastors, non-profit, marketplace and government leaders

   - 2-4 hour vision-cast, breakfast, lunch or afternoon coffee

Kingdom Forum:
   - Releasing the synergy of collaboration A diversity of kingdom leaders sharing vision for their community

Consulting:
   - Ideas, inputs & evaluation for city leadership teams

Speaking:
   - Citywide gatherings, forums, conferences, Sunday services

TOM WHITE
City Movement Consultant

tbwhite07@gmail.com
541-760-0126

Frontline Ministries
PO Box 786
Corvallis OR 97339

"one...
so that the
world will
believe"
Jn 17:21

FRONTLINE
catalyzing kingdom communities

Appendices

A Sampling of City Transformational Strategies

Under the sovereign leading of the Holy Spirit, commencing in the mid to late 1980's, we saw a variety of "early adopters" begin to articulate and activate a fresh vision of the Body of Christ working together in local communities. Through different "grids" (spiritual gifts, callings, skill-sets), these early pioneers each brought a unique interpretation of the creative work of the Holy Spirit unfolding in cities. It is therefore no surprise that we see today a variety of interpretations and "translations" that define this newly emergent paradigm. In the early stages we referred to this as "city-reaching." Then, the phrase "city transformation" was popularized. Today, many are referring to "city gospel movements." The descriptive language we use is of secondary importance. What is primary is that we understand, rightly interpret and contextually apply this dynamic increase of God's reign in our cities.

Here's a snapshot of some of these varied approaches:

Approaches to Community Transformation

- Presence-Based
- Evangelism
- Biblical Justice
- Marketplace Initiatives
- Church Partnerships
- Prayer/Power Evangelism
- "Gospel Movements"

We are seeing numerous contributors with unique and distinct approaches employed to catalyze the measurable transformation of both individuals and institutions. In any given city, such approaches may inform and shape one another, and work synergistically to bring release of kingdom presence and power in all spheres of societal endeavor.

I simply want to provide here a simple survey of the landscape of this paradigm, briefly highlight the distinctive feature of each approach, and identify one or two leading proponents representing that strategy. The list above is certainly not comprehensive, but rather representative of the diversity of approaches currently in play. Let's also understand there are no hard, impermeable lines that separate these approaches. There are numerous models that are "hybrids," where distinctive strategies are mixed together with varied degrees of emphasis. Remember, this is a paradigm in process, with considerable cross-fertilization of ideas crossing lines.

Proponents of the Presence-Based approach may be characterized as having a purity and fervency for the manifest presence of God that transforms life from the ordinary to extraordinary. They strongly eschew human effort, and are insistent on discerning and conforming to the ways of God revealed in Scripture. George Otis, Jr, Founder and Director of Sentinel Group, would be the leading proponent of an approach that places supernatural power as the source and sustainer of societal change. I was personally present at the very first showing of the *Transformations I* video in Santa Rosa, CA, in June, 1999, a watershed moment in the development of this paradigm. The *Transformations* video stories have stirred a fresh hope over the possibility of what the Spirit of God could do in any city where the hearts of the saints were aligned more fully with his purposes. Otis describes what he sees as three phases of divine transformation:

1. **Invitation**, a seeking and summoning of God's presence,
2. **Breakthrough**, initial visitations of the Spirit, and
3. **Transformation**, which he most recently has described as "transforming revival.

I want to commend Otis and his international network of transformational partners for their earnest, unwavering belief that if God's people, in any place, get their hearts right with one another, humble themselves in prayer, and align themselves fully with God's purposes, then the Spirit will deliver us from our ordinary endeavors and demonstrate his extraordinary power to change life as we know it.

The video produced by Sentinel that I find the most valuable is *The Quickening,* a brilliant fifty minute piece that most clearly defines what "transformation" is and is not, and presents the key principles Otis considers imperative for a transformational process to occur.

There are many among us who, when "cut," will bleed Evangelism, a passion for bringing unredeemed souls into the kingdom. While the "e" word finds little use these days, the priority of presenting the gospel relevantly and contextually is re-emerging. And while the day of the full blown, high budget citywide or regional "crusade" has clearly passed, the Luis Palau Evangelistic Association has pioneered a unique model that can be custom-made for city movements. Beginning in its home city of Portland, OR, the Palau organization worked in partnership with numerous local congregations and organizations to hold its first "Festival" in 1999 in Portland's Riverfront Park, a creative mosaic of music, ministry and preaching of the gospel.

The concept got traction, and spread to other cities. The leadership of Mission Houston engaged the Palau team in dialogue and planning, with the intent of maximizing sustainable kingdom impact. "Service days" preceding the Festival were built in, focused mostly on repairing and refurbishing the physical plants of local schools. This approach then morphed into a "season of service," mobilizing volunteers from churches to engage in practical projects. This hybrid model was so effective, the Palau organization re-tooled its approach, built in the "season of service" component, and held a second citywide Festival in Portland in 2008. This is an excellent example of a collaboration forged between kingdom assets from the *outside* of a city and gate-keeping leaders *inside* the city, who remain on the ground long after an event has come and gone. This approach also brings a healthy balance of the sharing of the good news with the doing of good works. The Palau organization has launched a website, www.gospelmovements.com, a vehicle for cities to share their stories, lessons learned, breakthroughs and challenges.

Another leading proponent in this genre is Dr. Paul Cedar, a world-class elder statesman of personal evangelism. As leader of the Mission America Coalition, Paul is stewarding a bold, broad vision, "Love 2020." Designed as neither program nor plan, this is a call to all Christians to cultivate a sustainable lifestyle of praying, caring for, and allowing the Holy Spirit to open doors for sharing the gospel with family, neighbors, co-workers and acquaintances (www.love2020.com). Paul writes, "This vision is so vast that it will be accomplished only by a great movement of the Holy Spirit through humble and dedicated followers of Jesus. Our vision for LOVE2020 is for every person in America to be loved by at least one Christ follower, who is living a prayer-care-share lifestyle, by year-end 2020."

Another proponent of personal evangelism that merits a highlight is Steve Sjogren (*Conspiracy of Kindness, 101 Ways to Reach Your Community*). Steve and his wife Janey carry a passion for people that is winsome and contagious! They bring to the mix a toolkit of ideas for softening and opening hearts to the gospel. In the 2012 edition of the prayer booklet *Seek God for the City,* co-authors Steve Hawthorne and Steve Sjogren share excellent, simple, do-able ways to "pray our way into people's stories."

The proponents of Biblical Justice carry an Isaiah 58 prophetic burden of compassion, a priority to meet the felt needs of the poor, broken and marginalized. John Perkins, African-American elder statesman, emerged from a crucible of suffering in the 1960's civil rights movement. John is a principal leader emeritus of the Christian Community Development Association. In his lecture at the 2010 National City Impact Roundtable in Birmingham, Alabama, John challenged delegates to be open to make radical, concrete adjustments to their lifestyles: being willing to re-locate (move into a neighborhood broken and in need of repair) and to re-distribute wealth, (the "haves" intentionally and sacrificially sowing resources into the lives of the "have-nots"). In short, a modern day application of Acts 2:44, 45. John is clear: he is not encouraging hand-outs, but rather wanting to empower those who are marginalized by systemic poverty break out of a victim mentality, and have opportunity to improve their lives. Perkins and his proponents are seriously working to implement the Isaiah 58 mandate. There are numerous other contextual expressions of social justice operative in cities, e.g., Love in the Name of Christ (Love, INC), Someone Cares (Houston), Love and Care (Abilene).

As I'm engaged in numerous conversations with leaders in many cities, I always find innovative pastors who initiate relationships with other pastors and congregations. **Proponents of Church Partnerships are passionate about selective, purposeful partnerships.** At the 2012 Movement Day in New York, Dr. Mac Pier shared the following: "What we're encouraging is an alliance of churches collaborating with world class partners around a big idea." Here's the trend: congregations and, in some cases, non-profit organizations working together on specific projects. In most cases, the impetus for this traces to relationships of trust between the senior pastors. In this era where we are de-emphasizing differences and celebrating common mission, this model is getting traction. Most often this involves either mega-church congregations (with an interest in broader impact), or congregations of influence, merging volunteer personnel and resources. A major contributor to this approach has been Eric Swanson, author of *The Externally Focused Church*. In 2010, Eric co-authored with colleague Sam Williams the ground breaking work *To Transform a City,* sharing additional examples of churches partnering together.

Recently, in January 2012, a cadre of leaders of influence in the greater Phoenix area launched "Undivided." Their Mission: One Church Serving the Valley. Their Vision: No Child Uncared for in the Valley. Their Strategy: Adopt every school, Eradicate hunger, Empty foster care. Friends, this is a *"big idea!"* The power of collaborative partnerships like this is clearly on the radar in communities all across the world.

Proponents of Marketplace Initiatives are often marked by a passion to engage their energy and resources in concrete projects that result in measurable outcomes. If we rightly understand the Body of Christ as a "royal priesthood," the arbitrary lines drawn between church, non-profit and marketplace fade away. Business leaders, by nature and gifting, engage with a well-defined project, are eager to roll up their sleeves and get working, and want to see results. So we're seeing numerous initiatives originating from movers in the marketplace aimed at societal transformation.

Since the departure of Bill Bright, Campus Crusade for Christ has undergone substantial organizational change, re-branding as "Cru" and balancing their work on campuses with an intentional emphasis on cities. Dr. Robert Varney, Ph.D. physicist turned kingdom strategist, leads a global think tank of international CCC leaders, Leader Led Movements, seeking to understand the complex, interwoven systems of city cultures, and how to communicate the gospel into the mindset of urban dwellers. Further, Cru's Dave Robinson is one of the key innovators and leaders of "Cru City ," a ministry devoted to kingdom citizens advancing the mission of Jesus for the well-being of their city. Here's their core passion: seeing people living wholly surrendered to Jesus, in community and on mission everyday.

Practitioners working in the Prayer/Power Evangelism group are characterized by a radical dependence on the Holy Spirit and his gifts to open doors to the hearts of "pre-Christians." Back in the early days of the Vineyard movement, John Wimber authored *Power Evangelism,* a first of its kind work emphasizing the power gifts of the Holy Spirit that operate in personal evangelism. My second book published in 1993, *Breaking Stronghholds: How Spiritual Warfare Sets Captives Free,* was my own contribution to this topic. There has been a resurgence of the Vineyard approach through the teaching ministry of Bill Johnson, pastor of Bethel Church, in Redding, CA. Through Bethel's School of Supernatural Ministry, many have been trained in learning to move in gifts of knowledge, prophecy, discernment and healing, gifts that expose needs of people, and open their hearts for the gospel. This approach has much to commend it, especially when reading the book of Acts.

Ed Silvoso (Harvest Evangelism) also brings an approach that fits in this category of "power evangelism." Ed continues to develop and apply the material he first presented in *That None Should Perish*. In recent years, he has preferred to work more with marketplace leaders, mobilizing personal prayer for the lost. Ed is very high on the value of prayer walking neighborhoods and places of business, placing prayer tents at fairs and festivals, etc.

So, lastly, we come to Gospel Movements, the most recent contribution to the transformational paradigm, men and women who possess a dual passion to lead with the gospel message, being intentional to get out of the Lords' way, carefully stewarding a God-breathed movement. Since the "city reaching" paradigm was birthed in the late 1980's, we have seen many pioneers and approaches emerge with new ideas and energies focused on advancing God's kingdom in specific places. "Movement Day," launched in the Fall 2010, is an annual gathering of practitioners of city movements in New York.. Under the spiritual tutelage of Dr. Tim Keller and others, leaders in New York are developing an understanding of the gospel as an "eco-system," a holistic synergy of kingdom influence that catalyzes spiritual, social and economic change. At all levels, life in any metropolitan environment is complex. There are systems within systems (marriage and family, race relations, education, health care, commerce) that affect one another. God forgive us if we have a truncated view of the gospel of Jesus Christ. God help us understand with greater depth the transformational power of his Word and Spirit that followers of Jesus can release into a city environment. I serve on the Leadership

Cabinet for Movement Day, and am personally engaged in this five year journey.

In June, 2013, I was invited by Mac Pier, Senior Associate of the Lausanne Movement, to participate in the Global Leadership Forum in Bangalore, India. The Holy Spirit led our working group on city movements to launch the Global Urban Leaders Learning Community (GULLC), an international association of practitioners and theologians committed to learning and applying more effectively what the Spirit of God is doing in city movements. Goals include hosting a global "Movement Day" congress in 2016 in New York inviting international city transformational movements, and launching a state-of-the-art web presence by Spring, 2014.

Summary

As this paradigm continues to grow, we desperately need the wisdom of Solomon:

> "Unless the Lord builds the house, its builders labor in vain. Unless the Lord watches over the city, the watchmen stand guard in vain" (Ps. 127:1).

We are seeing the emergence of a variety of approaches to "city transformation," and a diversity of contextual applications. This is encouraging. As I've shared throughout The Practitioner's Guide, God the Father is bringing forth concrete answers to Jesus' prayer for a John 17 "witness of oneness" among his followers. In walking this out, let's understand there is not a "one style and one size" approach that fits all situations. The Spirit of God is creative, and each city environment offers unique variables. Let's continue to honor and bless one another's endeavors in this arena of kingdom expansion, and allow Jesus, the Lord of every city, to continue to grow this kingdom wineskin in his way, in his time, and for his purposes.

Appendix

To Transform a City

How do you know if you're reaching a city?
Tim Keller | posted 3/07/2011

Tim Keller, pastor of Redeemer Presbyterian Church in Manhattan, recently spoke to New York City church leaders about something that concerns them all: reaching the city for Christ. Leadership editor Marshall Shelley was there, and after you read this article, read Shelley's interview with Tim Keller and Bill Hybels *"Leadership in the City."* This article is a condensed version of Keller's remarks. The complete talk can be found at http://movementday.com/604162.ihtml

It takes a movement to reach a city. Reaching an entire city takes more than having some effective churches even having a burst of revival energy and new converts.

Today, in almost every city in the world, some churches are growing. Some may be growing rapidly, and it's right to feel that God is doing great things in those churches.

People are coming to Christ. But it's another thing to ask: Is God reaching that city? If a few churches are growing, for instance, but the overall number of Christians is flat, is that city being reached for God?

Church growth often happens through "church reconfiguration," people from less vital or hurting churches going to more vigorous congregations. Now this isn't bad, because often in those more vigorous churches, Christians are being more well deployed. Perhaps a strong Christian woman is going to a hurting church—she loves her church, but there are fights and difficulties—and she can't bring her non-Christian friends to that church because the atmosphere is so unhealthy. So finally, with a heavy heart, she leaves and goes to the growing church in town, where she brings a non-Christian friend who finds faith in Christ at that church. That's all good. And yet, is that reaching a city? No.

What it takes to reach a city is a city-wide gospel movement, which means the number of Christians across the city is growing faster than the population, and therefore, a growing percentage of the people of that city are connecting with gospel-centered churches and are finding faith in Jesus Christ. That will eventually have an impact on the whole life of the city. That's what I mean by a city-wide gospel movement.

A citywide gospel movement is an organic thing. It's an energy unleashed across not only the city but across the different denominations, and therefore, there's no one church, no one organization, no one leader in charge of it all. It's bigger than that. It's the Holy Spirit moving across the whole city and as a result the overall body of Christ is growing faster than the population, and the city is being reached. And there's an impact for Christ made in the whole city.

The core of the movement

There are three layers to this kind of influence. At the core of this kind of movement is the first layer: a *contextualized biblical* gospel theology. Where do I get this? From the Book of Acts, from reading the history of revivals, and from my own experience here in New York. By "a biblical gospel," I mean a God-ordained third way between legalistic moralism and licentious relativism. When Paul writes to the Romans and rolled out the gospel, he first clarifies, "Look at the Gentiles, the pagans, who are living according to their own desires. That's not the gospel." Then he says, "And look at those who are living according to the Law of Moses. They've missed the gospel too."

Historically the Christian church, as Martin Luther expressed it, "is like a drunk man who, having fallen off the horse on one side, gets back up and falls off on the other."

Most Bible believing Christians today assume the main way you can lose the gospel is on the side of liberalism, relativism, the idea that you don't have to accept everything in the Bible, because it undermines biblical authority. Yes, that loses the gospel. But on the other side is legalism and moralism and Phariseeism. In 2008 during the presidential campaign, a guy got up and said to the candidates: "I've got one question to ask, and if you answer this question, I'll know everything I need to know about you: Do you believe every word of the Bible is true?"

That man's perspective is wrong. While I agree that it's very important to believe that every word in the Bible is true, both Jesus and the Pharisees agreed with that. You can believe that every word in the Bible is true and be lost, absolutely lost, as the Pharisees were. The church loses its life-changing dynamism to the degree that its theology goes off to this side or that side—into either uptight legalistic moralism, or into latitudinarianism, broadness, not believing the Bible, licentiousness, relativism.

By saying the biblical gospel is in the middle, that's not saying "moderation in all things." Jesus wasn't moderate in anything. He was radically gentle and radically truth loving at the same time. The gospel isn't a kind of middle-of-the-road, lukewarm thing. But the gospel is neither legalism nor licentiousness. And to the degree we lose the biblical gospel, we're never going to be a movement that reaches the city.

The core of the movement is also a *contextualized gospel.* Contextualization has not so much to do with theology as with culture. So, for example, recently I was talking to a young Christian woman who had moved to New York City years ago with her family from another country and grew up in a wonderful ethnic church. But eventually she became frustrated with that church because, as she said, "It was more important for them to stay inside their culture than to reach out to the rest of New York.

The only people who would ever find faith in that church were people who were absolutely like everybody from my homeland." They refused to assimilate, to adapt to the fact that they're in New York. Everything was so culturally narrow that the only people who would ever find faith there were people who had just gotten off a plane or a boat.

That's a failure to adapt, failure to contextualize. Paul said, "I've become all things to all people. I'm a Jew to the Jew; I'm a Greek to the Greek, in order that all people will receive the gospel."

Of course, you can over-adapt. To adapt too much to the culture of New York City is to adapt to worldliness, sin, greed, and idolatry. So where do you find that middle ground, where we contextualizing to the culture around us so that people there will hear the gospel, but we're not capitulating culturally? Ah, that's the area of wisdom. That's a contextualized biblical gospel theology. That's the first layer.

New churches tend to reach non-Christians at a rate 5-7 times the rate of older churches.

Around that core, for this to be a city-wide gospel movement, there's a second layer. We need a number of church multiplication movements within different denominations: new churches being planted and churches being renewed among the Baptists and Presbyterians and Pentecostals and Episcopalians and Lutherans and so on. (Sorry if I left somebody out, but there are about 26,000 Protestant denominations). Cities are diverse, and for reasons that only God knows, not everybody in New

York who wants to become a Christian will want to be a Presbyterian. Hard as that is to believe! And not everybody is going to be Pentecostal. Or Baptist.

For some reason God uses different denominational traditions to reach all sorts of people. And unless multiple denominations are flourishing, you don't reach a city.

Those distinctives are important. I hope that you really are what you are! And yet, for a city-wide movement, we can't be so tribal that you're a Presbyterian first and a Christian second. You're a Christian first and everything else second. You're a Christian first, and not only are you a Baptist or a Presbyterian second, you're a Christian first and you're a white or a Black or Asian or a Hispanic second.

In a city in which the body of Christ is so divided by denominations that they do not help each other, they do not work together, and therefore there isn't a dynamism that works across denominational barriers, you're not going to reach a city.

When I say "multiplication movement," I mean you are part of a multiplication movement if half the churches in your network are planting another church every five years. Then you're moving, because new churches grow and reach non-Christians in a way that older churches do not. Listen, my church is 21 years old, and we do not reach non-Christians the way we did in the first five years. That's just the way it is. New churches tend to reach non-Christians at a rate 5-7 times the rate of older churches. Why? It's just the way God

Appendix

works. There are sociological reasons, too. New churches are more focused on people outside: how are we going to reach out? As churches get older, they focus more on the needs of the people inside.

We need new churches if the body of Christ overall in a city is going to grow, new churches in a variety of traditions, denominations, and networks.

A ministry ecosystem

The third layer around the two inner rings is the most complex layer, and I

Consider seven kinds of ministry networks that interrelate with the churches. Some people call these parachurch or specialty ministries. But at least seven of these are an important part of the city-reaching ecosystem.

1. **City-wide prayer.** Revivals always happen with extraordinary prayer, uniting for the city, for one another.

2. **Specialist evangelism, movements reaching people of various ages, locations, stages, nationalities, religions.** The local church is a generalist place. We need help with youth, students, the business community, artists, and people of different faiths.

3. **Justice and mercy.** In order to tackle the problems of the city, to reach out to the poor, to

demonstrate the gospel to those who haven't seen it, we need those specializing in justice and mercy initiatives.

4. **Vocational faith/work initiatives.** We need the artists coming together, the media people coming together, the business types, the educators, etc. Almost always this has to happen across denominations for them to know one another and to form schools of thought on how faith affects the way in which we do our work.

5. **Institutions that support the family in the city.** In New York City, the Jewish community has done an excellent job of supporting family life. The community centers, the schools, the networks make it possible to stay in the city and raise families there.

6. **Institutions for theological training.** We need a leadership pipeline that goes from the campus to the youth to the campus through the churches very quickly and expertly prepares people theologically for ministry.

7. **Christian leaders coming together.** When the leaders of churches and ministries have enough unity and opportunity to network, we can help each other. We can discuss and discern what other areas of the city we need to be reaching. That overcomes tribalism and contributes to the greater good.

Appendix

This is what I mean by an ecosystem. It's a symbiotic relationship between the churches, which supply the people for these ministries, and the ministries, which produce people for the churches. These are interactive, interdependent forces that propel the movement forward.

When all these elements are in place, you have a gospel movement. You begin to see growth and change that goes beyond any one group, church, or network.

A whole city tipping point

When a gospel movement is underway, it may be that the Body of Christ develops to the point that a whole city tipping point is reached. By that I mean the moment when the number of gospel-shaped Christians in a city reaches critical mass. The Christian influence on the civic and social life of the city—on the very culture—is recognizable and acknowledged. That means between 10 and 20 percent of the population.

For example, neighborhoods stay largely the same if new types of residents (richer, poorer, or culturally different from the rest) comprise less than 5 percent of the population. But when the number of new residents reaches somewhere between 5 and 20 percent, depending on the culture, the whole neighborhood ethos shifts.

Prison ministers report that if more than 10 percent of the inmates become Christians, it changes the corporate culture of the prison. The relationships between prisoners, between prisoners and guards—all change.

In New York City, some groups have a palpable effect on the way life is lived when their numbers reach at least 5 to 15 percent and when the members are active in public life.

Manhattan starts to tip

We did some research about church growth in Manhattan. Twenty years ago there were approximately 1.1 million people and about 100 evangelical churches from the Upper West Side / Upper East Side down to the tip of Manhattan. Twenty years later there are about 200 evangelical churches.

Twenty years ago, less than 1 percent of Manhattan residents, 9,000 people, were in those churches. Today, it's over 3 percent, some 35,000 people. Our church, Redeemer Presbyterian, which is a big church, has planted a lot of churches. But it's exciting for us to realize that we have been directly involved with, at most, a quarter of those new churches.

In other words, something is going on in New York that goes beyond one church, one network, or any one denomination. It goes beyond any particular race or ethnic

We're a long way from getting to the place we need to be, a city tipping point, when 10 to 20 percent of the population goes to those churches, and you begin to realize that the whole city, the whole culture is going to change because of the impact of Christians in a place like New York.

That's what we're after. It takes a movement to reach a city, and that's more than just planting a church, or even seeing your denomination growing.

I'm praying that people will become part of a city-wide gospel movement, here in New York if you're here, or that God will raise up people who will pray for the same thing in the city where you live right now.

What Is a City?

The main Hebrew word translated "city" refers to any human settlement surrounded by a fortification or wall. Most ancient cities numbered only about 1,000-3,000 in population. "City," therefore, meant not so much population size as density.

Psalm 122:3 refers to this density:" Jerusalem, built as a city should be, closely compact." The word translated "compact" meant to be closely intertwined and joined. In a fortified city, the people lived close to one another in tightly compacted houses and streets. In fact, most ancient cities were estimated to be five to ten acres, with 240 residents per acre. By comparison, contemporary Manhattan houses only 105 residents per acre.

In ancient times, then, a city was what would today be called a "mixed use" walkable human settlement. Because of the population's density, there were places to live and work, to buy and sell, to pursue and enjoy art, to worship and to seek justice—all within an easy walk. In ancient times, rural areas and villages could not provide all these elements, and in our modern time, the "suburb" deliberately avoids this pattern. Suburbs are defined by single-use zones—so places to live, work, play, and learn are separated from one another and are reachable only by car, usually through pedestrian-hostile zones.

What makes a city a city is proximity. It brings people—and therefore residences, workplaces, and cultural institutions—together. It creates street life and marketplaces, bringing about more person-to-person interactions in a day than are possible anywhere else. This is what the biblical writers meant when they talked about a "city."—Tim Keller

Copyright © 2011 by the author or Christianity Today International/*Leadership* Journal.

Appendix

"Reading Your City"

Adapted from a Paper Written by Dr. Glenn Smith, Christian Direction, Montreal, CANADA

What follows is a select portion of Glenn Smith's paper that deals with an overview of contextualization of the gospel, and societal transformation. I have selected ten of Glenn's twenty steps that are very useful for engaging the endeavor of "reading your city."

The second voice: Christian traditions

The second theme that informs community research is our *Christian traditions,* meaning our study of the narratives of Scriptures, history and theology. Now the hermeneutical process becomes a true exchange between gospel and context. We come to the authoritative message with an exegetical method enabling us to understand a biblical theology of place. We ask, "What does God say through Scripture regarding this particular context?" This initial dialogue sets us off on a long process in which the more we understand the context, the more fresh readings of the Bible will arise. Scripture illuminates life, but life also illuminates Scripture. This dialogue must also include the practitioners' own perspectives and that of the community in which they base their initiatives.

Biblical and social hermeneutics conceived in this fashion represent a holistic enterprise in which the Holy Spirit guides the interpreters to a more complete reading and understanding of Scripture and a more complete understanding of their context.

There is an ongoing mutual engagement of the essential components of the process. As they interact, they are mutually adjusted. In this way, we come to Scripture with the relevant questions and perspectives. This results in a more attentive ear to the implications of the exegetical process, and a resulting theology that is more biblical and more pertinent to the culture. As we move from the cultural context through our own evolving worldview to the Bible and back to the context, we adopt increasingly relevant local reflection and initiatives. As we listen to Scripture and walk through our various situations in life, we are faced with a question: How can we hear and apply God's word in our cities and neighborhoods? In reality, the complexity of our communities means we constantly ask these questions. Holding text and context together is vital as we continue in an era of rapid urban growth, urbanization and globalization.

Contextualization and Transformation

The word contextualization literally means a "weaving together." For our purposes, it implies the interweaving of Scriptural teaching about "place" and the church within a particular human situation— the context. The very word focuses attention on the role of context in the theological enterprise. In a very real sense, all doctrinal reflection from the Scriptures is related in one way or another to the situation from which it was born, while addressing the aspirations, concerns, priorities and needs of the local group of Christians who are presently doing the reflection.

The task of contextualization is the essence of theological reflection. The challenge is to remain faithful to God's revelation and the historic texts of Scripture while being mindful of today's realities. An interpretative bridge is built between the Bible and its context to the circumstances of the local group of Christians who are doing the reflection. This is never a simple linear exercise. In this process, we approach the texts with humility and deep desire to keep on discovering their meaning. The first step of the hermeneutic exercise involves establishing what the text meant at the time it was written: what it meant "then." The second step involves creating the bridge to understanding the text in meaningful terms for the interpreters today: what it means "*now.*" The final step is to determine the meaning and application for those who will receive the message in their particular circumstances as the present day interpreters become ambassadors of the Good News: what it means "here." *Contextualization is not just for the one communicating, nor about the content that will be passed along. It is always concerned about what happens once we have communicated—about the ultimate impact of the message on the audience.*

For what purpose does the practitioner pursue contextualization? Why listen to both the present context and Christian tradition, including our study of the Scriptures, Church history and theology? Increasingly, we hear the use of the word *transformation* as a term that encompasses all that the church does as followers of Jesus in God's mission in the city. But what does this mean? What does it entail? Inspired by the South African missiologist, John de Gruchy's reflections, I suggest that a transformed place is that kind of community that pursues fundamental changes, a stable future, and the sustaining and enhancing of all of life rooted in a vision bigger than mere urban politics. He adds that "it is an open-ended multi- layered process, *at once social and personal,* that is energized by hope, yet rooted in the struggles of the present." John W. de Gruchy, *Christianity, Art and Transformation: Theological Aesthetics in the Struggle for Social Justice* (Cambridge: Cambridge University Press, 2001), 3

Steps towards understanding your context

To begin the process of reading one's community, let me propose some concrete steps. These are best undertaken by teams—usually ecumenical "task forces"—that try to understand their community context. After the "exegesis" or community assessment, it will be important to prioritize the initiatives that congregations will undertake.

Appendix

1. **Compile a list of significant historical events** that inform the community's identity. These could be specific, historic conflicts that took place, such as a war or dispute, specific unifying events such as the city coming together to fight a massive fire, specific decisions that leaders made such as the building of a community centre, or something that happened that gave people hope, such as a person doing something heroic or selfless. These will provide clues to the best way for the church to focus its energy. Begin this step by reading about the community. The local library or historical society is where we always begin.

2. **Study the growth patterns of the city.** One can find this information in libraries, city councils, museums, bookstores, local newspapers and on local websites.

   - Why is the city growing (or why did it grow)?
   - Who are (and were) the immigrants to the city?
   - Where did they come from and where are they settled?
   - Where are they employed? (Understand clearly the sections or zones that make up the city:
     - Downtown
     - Blue dollar neighbourhoods
     - Ethnic neighbourhoods
     - Industrial Zones
     - Commercial Areas

3. **Study the neighborhoods: their ethnic, social and economic composition,** religious affiliations, occupational patterns, younger and older populations, concentrations of the elderly, young professionals singles, and problem groups. *To understand a neighborhood you must walk the streets and talk to people, insiders and outsiders. Census data is important, but on site observation is best.* People groups crisscross in the community. Probe to discover the dominant influence in a neighborhood: is it ethnic identity? Social class? Undertake a participant-observer approach.

Examine census maps if they are available. Find out from city planners and real estate offices where city populations are expected to move, where commercial and industrial zones will develop, and which areas are slated to undergo major changes. Isolate the sectors of your larger community using the wheel diagram of the city on page x. This represents the functions of a city.

What is the extent of social contact between the different people groups? Is social contact increasing? Take time to chat with residents and pedestrians in the area. Ask them what the most significant changes are that they see or experience in the neighborhood. When walking the streets, watch for the impact of these population shifts on the neighborhood.

Appendix

Many congregations use prayer walks as a way to learn more about their community.

4. **Determine and analyze the power centres** in the community: the political figures, the police department, the business leaders and the Chamber of Commerce, the religious leaders. Who controls the media—TV, radio, the newspapers? Who controls commerce and finance? The schools and the arts? What are the religious and moral commitments of the people in positions of power?

5. **Analyze the felt needs of specific people groups** within the community. You are looking for indications of receptivity and "keys" which may unlock doors to homes and hearts. Felt needs vary from group to group. In some communities, such things as personal illness, loneliness, physical hardships, insecurity in terms of housing, property rights, and the threat of losing one's dwelling are very real. In other neighborhoods, the felt needs may be entirely different.

Once a church has demonstrated a commitment to helping meet people's felt needs, and a bridge of relational trust has been established, there is often a greater openness to a discussion of deeper, spiritual needs, and to Christ who meets all needs.

6. **Examine the traffic flow.** Just as successful advertisers know where to place their signs, practitioners need to know where to begin their ministries, where they can readily be seen and reached.

Find out where each of the following is located:
- community service centres
- libraries
- police stations
- fire stations
- city hall
- shopping centres
- sports facilities

7. **Who are the idea-people,** the opinion-makers? Subscribe to the weekly publications in the area. Read it faithfully. Get conversant with local radio and TV reporters and personalities to discover how news and opinion spreads in the community, and in particular groups.

8. **Examine the relationship between city-dwellers and the rural,** small-town communities outside the city. Do certain segments of the urban population maintain strong ties with their rural cousins? Is there a lot of travel and visiting between city and village? What are the present immigration patterns from the countryside? How might the urban-rural interaction be used for the spread of the gospel and multiplication of churches? Most of this information is available in census data.

9. **Ministries and churches in the community: locate** them on a map; identify them by denomination, size and age. What transformational ministries and social services are already taking place through these ministries and churches? Reflect on what the church map shows.

10. **If you are developing a church planting strategy,** analyze the various types of existing churches and para-church ministries in the city. Find out the growth patterns (if any) of the various churches: attendance, membership, and rate of growth. Try to determine the nature of the growth: is it by transfer, conversion, or by births? One can often locate this information by chatting with congregational leaders.

Inquire about church planting efforts and church closures in the past several years. Which churches have closed? Why? Who has started new churches, and why and where did they succeed? Learn all you can from them.

Who is planning to start new churches? Where, and among which people groups? Find out all you can from church and mission sources as to what is being planned for the community.

Strategies: what has been tried in the past, what has failed, and what was effective in starting churches and stimulating growth? Analyze the information you receive.

In the light of recent church growth studies, what has been "done right" in this community, and where ought things to have been done differently?

Christians and non-Christians: where are the Christians located (of course, this may not be where they attend church)? Identify areas of the city where relatively few Christians live. Identify Christians in positions of influence in the city: in business, politics, the media, education, entertainment, and sports. Analyze their potential for wider spread of the gospel and assistance in planting churches.

List and analyze the parachurch ministries (if any) operating in and to the community. How might each contribute something to the overall strategy? Are there some you may want to avoid because they might have a negative influence on church multiplication?

Make an inventory of all possible personnel resources that might be tapped for the carrying out of your church planting strategy. For example, are there Bible College or seminary students available to help with door-to-door calling? Could interns be borrowed from existing churches to help younger congregations?

Evaluate all known methods for church planting in light of what you know about this community—its history, people, existing churches, and particular characteristics. What methods have proven effective elsewhere and appear appropriate for this community—and are within the capabilities of your resources. List and evaluate the community agencies (private, religious and civic) that are designed to meet particular needs (literacy, overnight shelter, emergency food and clothing, and so on) and consider how their help can be incorporated into your overall strategy.

Appendix

Why a "City Church?"

Understanding How God Views the Church in Our City.

"I pray…for those who will believe in me through their message, that all of them may be one, Father, just as you are in me and I am in you.… I have given them the glory that you gave me, that they may be one as we are one.… May they be brought to complete unity to let the world know that you sent me and have loved them even as you have loved me." John 17:20-23

The following is a helpful, succinct, "snap-shot" answer to the question, Why a "City Church?" Formatted by Dr. David Niquette, Ft. Collins, CO)

The life, health and growth of the church of Jesus Christ immediately following Pentecost stands as one of the greatest demonstrations of God's grace and power throughout the centuries. A key factor that contributed to the effectiveness of the early church was the practical, relational unity of the people of God in any given city. The existence or absence of such unity in our cities today has important implications for effective ministry.

The church in our city already exists in the mind of God. It is not something we create or join. God calls pastors to each church in this city. By virtue of that divine call, each is a partner with other God-appointed pastors. We honor God when we support our ministry colleagues in reaching our city. God desires the whole church to reach the whole city with the whole gospel.

The Scriptural Basis for the "City-Church"

What is the biblically historical basis for developing a city-wide church partnership and strategy? Consider the New Testament data through a "city-lens" of vision:

A. Jesus dealt extensively with people in their city context.

1. **Unlike John the Baptist,** much of Jesus' ministry and miracles take place within cities and towns of Israel. A simple list of the places where Jesus is recorded to have exercised his ministry indicates that cities held an important place in Jesus' strategy of ministry (i.e. Nain, Nazareth, Cana, Korazin, Tyre, Sidon, Zarephath, Caesarea Philippi, Capernaum, Sychar, Bethany, Jericho, Jerusalem, etc.).

2. **The passion of the Lord for the city of Jerusalem** is undeniable in his words of Luke 13:34, "O Jerusalem, Jerusalem, you who kill the prophets and stone

those sent to you, how often I have longed to gather your children together as a hen gathers her chicks under her wings, but you were not willing!"

3. **Jesus himself prayed specifically for the unity** of all those who would believe on Him through the testimony of his disciples and indicated that such unity would be a powerful apologetic to a watching world (John 17:20-23).

4. **Jesus spoke some of his harshest words of judgment** against individual cities (Mt. 11:20ff) rather than provinces, regions or nation-states.

5. **Jesus called for effective world evangelization** to begin first with effective city-focused witness (Ac. 1:8). Note the relationship in Acts 2 and 4 between united city-church life and ongoing evangelistic witness and growth.

6. **Jesus, in the Parable of the Ten Minas** (Luke 19:11-27) rewarded faithful and competent stewards of mere financial resources with oversight of entire cities.

7. **Our Lord's last recorded words** to the developing churches of the first century were addressed to the spiritual needs of "the church [singular] in…" each of seven individual cities.

B. The Early Church understood "the church" in three distinct capacities.

1. **The Church Universal:** The entire community of believers in Christ through all ages, in diverse cultures and nations of whom each believer is a part but which does not have opportunity to gather together at one time (see Mt. 16:18; Ac. 9:31; 1 Cor. 15:9; Gal. 1:13; Eph. 1:22; 3:10,21; 5:23-25, 27, 29, 32; Phil. 3:6; Col. 1:18, 24).

2. **The City-Church:** The visible, interrelating, localized (within the same geographical city) community of persons who believed in Christ and periodically gathered together to fulfill mutual functions as believers. See for example, the church in Jerusalem (Acts 5:11; 8:1, 3; 11:22; 14:27; 15:4, 22), the church at Antioch (Acts 11:26; 13:1; 15:3, 30) the churches in Iconium, Lystra, and Pisidian Antioch (Acts 14:21-23), the church at Caessaria (Acts 18:22), the church at Ephesus (Acts 20:17; 1 Tim. 3:5, 15; 5:16, 17), the church in Cenchrea (Rm. 16:1), the church in Corinth (1 Cor. 1:2; 11:18; 14:23; 2 Cor. 1:1), the church at Philippi (Phil. 1:1; 4:15), the church at Laodicea (Col. 4:16; Rev. 3:14), the church at Thessalonica (1 & 2 Thess. 1:1) the other churches of Revelation (Rev. 2:1, 8, 12, 18; 3:1, 7) and other churches (Gal. 1:2; 3 John. 1:9, 10).

3. **The House Church: Believers** of a particular geographic area/city who frequently gathered

together in homes of other believers (Acts 12:5; Rm. 16:5; 1 Cor. 16:19; Col. 4:15; Phile. 1:2).

NOTE: Twentieth-century western Christianity has been quick to acknowledge both the church universal and the modern house/local church in Scripture but has given little or no attention to the city-church in the New Testament - that church which is referred to more often than either of the other two distinct church entities.

C. **The apostles viewed the city-church as the central representation of the Body of Christ in a given area.**

1. **By far the largest body of references to "church"** in the New Testament refer to the local city church (see 2.B. above). Most of the Epistles were written either to all the saints of a city (Eph. 1:1; Phil. 1:1; Col. 1:2) or to the city-church there (1 & 2 Cor., 1 & 2 Thess. and the churches of Revelation 2 & 3).

2. **When unity upon that city-wide basis** was threatened by factions who followed various spiritual leaders, Paul is forced to speak to them as "worldly, mere infants in Christ" (1 Cor. 3:1).

3. **Paul left Titus in Crete to "appoint elders in every town"** (Titus 1:5) rather than various gathered fellowships in a given city.

4. **Whenever Paul writes to saints in a given city,** he addressed his words to "the church" (singular) in that city but when he writes or refers to a region (such as Judea, Galatia or Macedonia) he speaks to/of "the churches" (plural) of that region.

Summary and Challenge: In the first century, it is evident that God dealt with His people at some level on a city-church basis, and His people lived in biblical unity at the city level. This seemed to be a crucial component of the effective spread of the Gospel.

What might be the impact on our city if spiritual leaders and churches worked together in a functional unity? What would happen if a significant number of congregations in this city mobilized together to reach the lost? If the Great Commission is to become reality in our city, it will require far more than any one church or denomination can possibly address. It will take . . .

The whole church reaching the whole city with the whole gospel!

Adapted and modified by David Niquette, Coordinator for Pastors Prayer Summits, Fort Collins Church Network, Inc. from "A Brief Apologetic for the City Church of Spokane" *by John S. Repsold.*

Appendix

Format for a 90 Minute Citywide Worship Gathering

I have found that an annual or semi-annual gathering dedicated to calling the citywide Body of Christ together to worship and intercede for the city releases something powerful in the Spirit. Keep this simple, focused on three things: 1) corporate worship, 2) intercession ("Thy kingdom come, Thy will be done in _____"), and 3) casting vision and raising funds for your movement. This model below has proven to be effective.

5:45   Begin Welcome and Communication Slides Rotating on Screen

6:00   Gathering Songs (2)

6:07   Welcome (from a city movement leader)

"Shout-outs," Churches present?

intro worship team

intro host pastor

6:10   Welcome (from the host pastor)

       welcome, seating, restrooms

       lead a corporate prayer (on-screen, e.g., Romans 15:5-7)

6:15   ADORATION (40 minutes of sustained worship)

       By 6:35, worship team segues into 2-3 songs that invite prayer for healing/ encouragement. Emcee opens the altar for personal prayer, with leaders available to pray alongside. Worship team continues with a song focused on consecration.

6:45   CONSECRATION (worship continues, inviting fresh consecration)

6:55   RELEASING GOD'S FAVOR INTO THE CITY

       There are a variety of ways to pray for your city. Here is one suggestion:

              move into mixed-church huddles of 6-8, take 1 minute to get acquainted

              30 secs…all recite Jer 29:7 together, on screen (or Is. 62:6, 7)

              pray 8-10 minutes, asking God to release shalom to youth, the poor, unsaved, local gov't officials, local businesses…creation of new jobs, etc. (worship team irrigates with soft instrumental, leads out with a chorus)

7:05　　EXALTATION (continue in worship, closing with "We Exalt Thee" (a capella)

7:15　　INVESTING IN THE CITY MOVEMENT

slides that communicate the vision/mission of your movement, citywide initiatives/projects, opportunities for involvement

upcoming things on the schedule

offering: challenge to invest in the "city church"

7:20　　CELEBRATION

Worship team closes with 2-3 "roof raisers."

7:30　　BENEDICTION/BLESSING

Appendix

Suggested Format & Guidelines for a Weekly One Hour Prayer Gathering For City Movement Leaders

Participants: Pastors, Associate Pastors, leaders of non-profits, marketplace leaders, men & women, multi-generational, multi-ethnic. Suggestion: poll prospective participants via e-mail: What are the times of your regular week that definitely do NOT work for you? Then select the least conflictive hour of the week.

Scriptural foundation: Is 62:1-6, Jer 29:7, 1 Tim 2. Primarily, this is intercessory prayer for an increase of God's kingdom in a city or region. Jesus' words apply here as well: "Thy kingdom come, thy will be done in _____ as it is in heaven." Secondarily, this gathering, over months and years, provides context for building a functional John 17 kingdom community, affirming, caring and praying for one another as friends.

Appoint a leader or leaders to oversee/facilitate. Any mature leader in your movement can facilitate, IF they understand the ground rules. (Corvallis and Kingston have one person responsible to recruit facilitators).

Recommend staying at one location for at least a year at a time with comfortable chairs, quiet room, ideally with side room and kitchen available for add-on informational or connection lunches.

Format:

- Facilitator defines the focus in first 10 min, 15 maximum (a visitor...a Scripture focus...a prayer target), then engage corporate prayer for at least 40 min.

- Can begin or close with a gifted minstrel leading 2-3 songs. It is helpful to "irrigate" this with worship any time, instrumental or voices only.

- Build in a variety of foci: mayor, police chief, school principal, someone in social services, a new pastor in town, leader of a serving ministry, university campus leader, etc.

- Utilize a variety of prayer formats: a) open corporate, b) small groups, c) personal silence/intercession, d) prayer walk, e) prayer chair in middle

Wrap up ON TIME, and allow 2-3 minutes at close for "kingdom announcements" (events, trainings, outreaches). *Be careful to not allow this to become a standard "trade show" where pastors and non-profits come mostly to "bring their stuff."* We allow only very brief announcements, and often have a table for voluntary pick up of promotional materials. Protect the main, plain purpose of this time to lift, thru agreement and faith, intercessory incense to fill the bowls of God's favor and blessing on the city/region (Ps. 141:2; Rev. 5:8 & 8:3).

Appendix

A "Short Form" Instruction for Prayerwalking

Prayerwalking is simply praying on-site with insight (observation) and inspiration (illumination from the Holy Spirit). It is a creative form of prayer that is visible, verbal and mobile. Its usefulness is twofold: 1) to gain spiritual reconnaissance of a neighborhood, a city or a nation, and 2) to release the power of God's Word and Spirit in specific places for particular people, and for specific concerns.

> "Be sure God is addressed, and people are blessed"
> Steve Hawthorne, author of Prayerwalking

I. PRAYERWALKING INVOLVES—

1. **Walking** ~ in pairs, triplets or small groups

2. **Worshiping** ~ extolling the Lord's names and nature

3. **Watching** ~ for outward clues (data from faces and places), and inward cues (discernment from the Holy Spirit)

II. PREPARATION

1. **Commit your walk** to the Lord & ask the Spirit to guide

2. **Cover yourselves** with divine protection (Ps. 91). Praying ground can quickly become a battleground.

3. **Connect with the Holy Spirit.** Only He can enable you and your team to offer prayer in alignment with the will and work of the Father (Ro. 8:26,27).

III. PRAYERWALK

1. **Mix and mingle** conversation with praise and praying

2. **Have freedom** to discreetly worship as you walk

3. **Speak Scripture** to release God's favor/ blessing (Jer.29:7)

4. **Ask the Holy Spirit** to direct your steps

   - Enter and walk through buildings
   - Linger in a particular place to observe and intercede
   - Stop and pray in particular places, or pray for specific people

IV. DE-BRIEF

1. **Glean**: what did we observe and discern?

2. **What did we experience?** Share mental impressions and emotions

3. **Were there any "divine appointments"** to thank the Lord for?

4. **What did we learn**, about the site we walked, about ourselves?

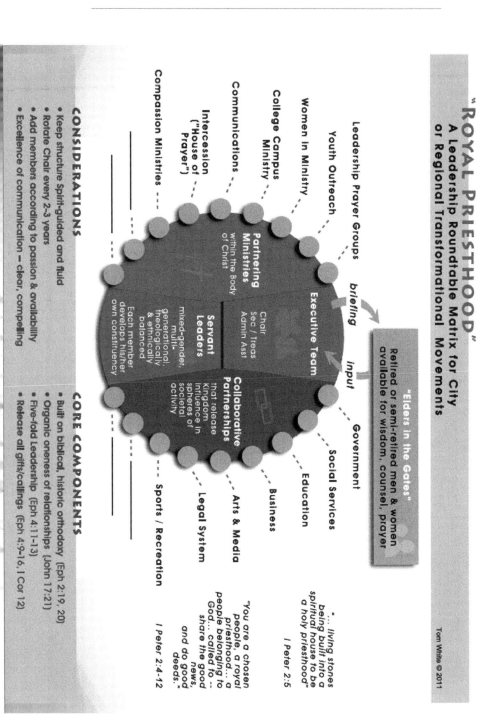

Footnotes

Chapter Two

1. **Keller, Tim,** *Center Church,* Zondervan, Grand Rapids, MI, 2012, p. 17.

2. **Greene, Brad,** *Seeking the Wholeness of the City,* Knoxville, TN, 2011, p. 7.

Chapter Three

1. **Yancy, Philip,** *Christianity Today,* Carol Stream, IL, November, 2008.

Chapter Four

1. **Greene, Brad,** *Seeking the Wholeness of the City,* Knoxville, TN, p. 20.

Chapter Six

1. **Hanleybrown, Kanie and Kramer,** *"Channeling Change: Making Collective Impact Work,"* Stanford Social Innovation Review, Stanford, CA, 2012.

Chapter Seven

1. **Hawkins, Greg, Parkinson,** Cally, MOVE, Zondervan, Grand Rapids, MI, 2011, p. 240.

2. **Broocks, Rice,** *"Evangelism is Back!"*, Charisma Magazine, Lake Mary, FL, July 2012.

3. **Sjogren,** *Seek God for Your City,* 2012, Austin, TX, 2012, p. 56.

4. Ibid, p. 58.

Chapter Eight

1. **White, Tom,** *The Believers Guide to Spiritual Warfare,* Regal, Ventura, CA, 2011, p. 179.

2. **McIntosh, Gary, Rima, Samuel,** *Overcoming the Darkside of Leadership,* Baker, Grand Rapids, Baker, 1997, p. 22.

3. **Barton, Ruth Haley,** *Strengthening the Soul of Your Leadership,* IVP Books, Downers Grove, IL, 2008, p. 43.

4. **Chambers, Oswald,** *My Utmost for His Highest,* Discovery House, Grand Rapids, MI, 1992, June 20.